CW00347607

AAT UNIT 2

MAKING AND RECORDING PAYMENTS

WORKBOOK

ISBN 1 85179 925 7

British Library Cataloguing-in-Publication data

A catalogue record for this book is available from the British Library.

We are grateful to the Association of Accounting Technicians for permission to reproduce past assessment material. The solutions have been prepared by The Financial Training Company.

Published by

The Financial Training Company
22J Wincombe Business Park
Shaftesbury
Dorset
SP7 9QJ

All rights reserved. No part of this publication may be reproduced, stored in a retrieval system, or transmitted, in any form or by any means, electronic, mechanical, photocopying, recording or otherwise, without the prior written permission of The Financial Training Company.

© The Financial Training Company 2001

Contents

	Page	
Preface	iv	

	Questions	Answers
Key techniques	1	237
Practice devolved assessment 1	57	*
Practice devolved assessment 2	89	263
Practice devolved assessment 3	105	*
Practice devolved assessment 4	121	275
Practice devolved assessment 5	141	*
Practice devolved assessment 6	151	283
Mock devolved assessment 1 questions	173	
Mock devolved assessment 1 answer booklet	197	
Mock devolved assessment 1 answers		*
Mock devolved assessment 2 questions	209	
Mock devolved assessment 2 answer booklet	217	
Mock devolved assessment 2 answers		293

* See Lecturers' Resource pack

Preface

This Workbook has been produced specifically for Unit 2 of the AAT's Education and Training Scheme

It is designed to complement the single textbook which covers Units 1, 2 and 3.

There are two similar workbooks which cover Units 1 and 3

The Workbook has the following features.

♦ A section of 'Key Techniques' which reinforce the main competencies which students must acquire to succeed at this unit.

♦ Six practice devolved assessments.

♦ Two mock devolved assessments.

♦ The answers to practice assessments 1, 3 and 5 and mock assessment 1 have been withheld from this Workbook following discussions with lecturers   These answers are available in the Lecturers' Resource Pack which is available to colleges who adopt our books.

KEY TECHNIQUES - QUESTIONS

Credit purchases: documents (covering Chapter 11)

Question 1

You work in the accounts department of Nethan Builders and given below are three purchase invoices together with the related purchase orders and delivery note You are to check each invoice carefully and note any problems or discrepancies that you find

---

INVOICE

A J Broom & Company Limited

Invoice to:
Nethan Builders
Brecon House
Stamford Road
Manchester
M16 4PL

59 Parkway
Manchester
M2 6EG
Tel 0161 560 3392
Fax 0161 560 5322

Deliver to:
As above

Invoice no	046123
Tax point	22 April 20X1
VAT reg no	661 2359 07
Purchase order no:	7164

Code	Description	Quantity	VAT rate %	Unit price £	Amount exclusive of VAT £
DGS472	SDG Softwood	9 6 m	17 5%	8 44	81 02
CIBF653	Joist hanger	7	17 5%	12 30	86 10
					167 12
Trade discount 10%					16 71
					150 41
VAT at 17 5%					26 32
Total amount payable					176 73

INVOICE

Invoice to:
Nethan Builders
Brecon House
Stamford Road
Manchester
M16 4PL

Deliver to:
As above

Jenson Ltd

30 Longfield Park
Kingsway
M45 2TP
Tel 0161 511 4666
Fax: 0161 511 4777

Invoice no	47792
Tax point	22 April 20X1
VAT reg no	641 3229 45
Purchase order no:	7162

Code	Description	Quantity	VAT rate %	Unit price £	Amount exclusive of VAT £
PL432115	Door lining set 32 × 115 mm	14	17 5%	30 25	423 50
PL432140	Door lining set 32 × 138 mm	8	17 5%	33.15	265.20

	688 70
Trade discount 15%	103 30
	585 40
VAT at 17 5%	102 44
Total amount payable	687 84

Deduct discount of 3% if paid within 14 days

INVOICE

Haddow Bros

Invoice to:
Nethan Builders
Brecon House
Stamford Road
Manchester
M16 4PL

Deliver to:
As above

The White House
Standing Way
Manchester
M13 6FH
Tel 0161 560 3140
Fax 0161 560 6140

Invoice no   033912
Tax point: 22 April 20X1
VAT reg no: 460 3559 71

Code	Description	Quantity	VAT rate %	Unit price £	Amount exclusive of VAT £
PLY8FE1	Plywood Hardwood 2440 × 1220 mm	12 sheets	17 5%	17 80	213 60
					213 60

VAT at 17 5%   36 63

Total amount payable   250 23

Deduct discount of 2% if paid within 10 days

PURCHASE ORDER

Nethan Builders

Brecon House
Stamford Road
Manchester
M16 4PL

To: Jenson Ltd
30 Longfield Park
Kingsway
M45 2TP

Tel   0161 521 6411
Fax.   0161 521 6412
Date: 14 April 20X1
Purchase order no   7162

Delivery address
(If different from above)

-

Invoice address
(If different from above)

-

Code	Quantity	Description	Unit price (exclusive of VAT) £
PL432140	8	Door lining set 32 × 138 mm	33.15
PL432115	14	Door lining set 32 × 115 mm	30.25

PURCHASE ORDER

Nethan Builders

Brecon House
Stamford Road
Manchester
M16 4PL
Tel·   0161 521 6411
Fax·   0161 521 6412
Date·   14 April 20X1
Purchase order no: 7164

To: A J Broom & Co Ltd
59 Parkway
Manchester
M2 6EG

Delivery address
(If different from above)

-

Invoice address
(If different from above)

-

Code	Quantity	Description	Unit price (exclusive of VAT) £
DGS472	9 6 m	SDG Softwood	8.44
CIBF653	5	Joist hanger	12.30

PURCHASE ORDER

Nethan Builders

Brecon House
Stamford Road
Manchester
M16 4PL
Tel·   0161 521 6411
Fax: 0161 521 6412
Date.   14 April 20X1
Purchase order no. 7165

To: Haddow Bros
The White House
Standing Way
Manchester
M13 6FH

Delivery address
(If different from above)

-

Invoice address
(If different from above)

-

Code	Quantity	Description	Unit price (exclusive of VAT) £
PLY8FE1	12 sheets	Plywood Hardwood 2440 × 1220 mm	17.80

DELIVERY NOTE

Jenson Ltd

30 Longfield Park
Kingsway
M45 2TP
Tel 0161 511 4666
Fax: 0161 511 4777

Deliver to:
Nethan Builders
Brecon House
Stamford Road
Manchester
M16 4PL

Delivery note no	771460	
Date:	19 April 20X1	
VAT reg no	641 3229 45	

Code	Description	Quantity	VAT rate %	Unit price £	Amount exclusive of VAT £
PL432115	Door lining set 32 × 115 mm	14			
PL432140	Door lining set 32 × 138 mm	8			

Goods received in good condition

Print name   C JULIAN

Signature   C Julian

Date   19/4/X1

DELIVERY NOTE

A J Broom & Company Limited

59 Parkway
Manchester
M2 6EG
Tel: 0161 560 3392
Fax 0161 560 5322

Deliver to:
Nethan Builders
Brecon House
Stamford Road
Manchester
M16 4PL

Delivery note no	076429
Date:	20 April 20X1
VAT reg no:	661 2359 07
Purchase order no	7164

Code	Description	Quantity	VAT rate %	Unit price £	Amount exclusive of VAT £
CIBF653	Joist hanger	7			
DGS472	SDG Softwood	9 6 m			

Goods received in good condition

Print name   C JULIAN

Signature   C Julian

Date   20/4/X1

DELIVERY NOTE

Haddow Bros

The White House
Standing Way
Manchester
M13 6FH
Tel 0161 560 3140
Fax: 0161 560 6140

Deliver to:
Nethan Builders
Brecon House
Stamford Road
Manchester
M16 4PL

Delivery note no   667713
Date: 17 April 20X1
VAT reg no: 460 3559 71

Code	Description	Quantity	VAT rate %	Unit price £	Amount exclusive of VAT £
PLY8FE1	Plywood Hardwood 2440 × 1220 mm	10			

Goods received in good condition

Print name   C JULIAN

Signature   C Julian

Date   17/4/X1

Question 2

Nethan Builders have also just received the following credit note   You are required to check that the credit note is clerically accurate

CREDIT NOTE

J M Bond & Co

Credit note to:
Nethan Builders
Brecon House
Stamford Road
Manchester
M16 4PL

North Park Industrial Estate
Manchester
M12 4TU
Tel: 0161 561 3214
Fax: 0161 561 3060

Credit note no	06192
Tax point	22 April 20X1
VAT reg no	461 4367 91
Invoice no:	331624

Code	Description	Quantity	VAT rate %	Unit price £	Amount exclusive of VAT £
DGSS4163	Structural Softwood Untreated	6 m	17 5%	6 85	41 10

	41 10
Trade discount 15%	8 22
	32 88
VAT at 17 5%	5 75
Total amount of credit	38 63

Credit purchases: primary records (covering Chapter 12)

Question 1

Nethan Builders analyse their purchases into wood, bricks and cement, and small consumables such as nails and screws   You are given three purchase invoices, recently received, to enter into the purchases day book given

An extract from the purchase ledger coding manual is given

Supplier	Purchase ledger code
A J Broom & Co Ltd	PL08
Jenson Ltd	PL13
Magnum Supplies	PL16

Today's date is 3 May 20X1

Enter the invoices into the analysed purchases day book and total each of the columns

---

INVOICE

MAGNUM SUPPLIES

Invoice to:
Nethan Builders
Brecon House
Stamford Road
Manchester
M16 4PL

140/150 Park Estate
Manchester
M20 6EG
Tel 0161 561 3202
Fax 0161 561 3200

Deliver to:
As above

Invoice no	077401
Tax point	1 May 20X1
VAT reg no:	611 4337 90

Code	Description	Quantity	VAT rate %	Unit price £	Amount exclusive of VAT £
BH47732	House Bricks – Red	400	17 5%	1 24	496 00

	496 00
Trade discount 15%	74 40
	421 60
VAT at 17 5%	72 30
Total amount payable	493 90

Deduct discount of 2% if paid within 10 days

INVOICE

Invoice to:
Nethan Builders
Brecon House
Stamford Road
Manchester
M16 4PL

Deliver to:
As above

A J Broom & Company Limited

59 Parkway
Manchester
M2 6EG
Tel: 0161 560 3392
Fax 0161 560 5322

Invoice no	046193
Tax point	1 May 20X1
VAT reg no	661 2359 07

Code	Description	Quantity	VAT rate %	Unit price £	Amount exclusive of VAT £
DGT472	SDGS Softwood 47 × 225 mm	11 2 m	17 5%	8 44	94 53
NBD021	Oval Wire Nails 100 mm	7 boxes	17 5%	2 50	17 50

	112 03
Trade discount 10%	11 20
	100 83
VAT at 17 5%	17 64
Total amount payable	118 47

INVOICE

Invoice to:
Nethan Builders
Brecon House
Stamford Road
Manchester
M16 4PL

Deliver to:
As above

Jenson Ltd

30 Longfield Park
Kingsway
M45 2TP
Tel: 0161 511 4666
Fax 0161 511 4777

Invoice no:	47823
Tax point	1 May 20X1
VAT reg no:	641 3229 45
Purchase order no:	7211

Code	Description	Quantity	VAT rate %	Unit price £	Amount exclusive of VAT £
PLY8FU	Plywood Hardboard	16 sheets	17 5%	17 80	284 80
BU611	Ventilator Brick	10	17 5%	8 60	86 00
					370 80

VAT at 17 5% — 62 94

Total amount payable — 433 74

Deduct discount of 3% if paid within 14 days

Purchases day book

Date	Invoice no	Code	Supplier	Total	VAT	Wood	Bricks/ Cement	Consumables

Question 2

Julian Hargreaves is a self-employed painter and decorator He uses an analysed purchases day book and analyses his purchases into paints, wallpaper and other purchases

Given below are three purchase invoices that he has received The purchase ledger codes for the three suppliers are

Mortimer & Co	PL03
F L Decor Supplies	PL06
Specialist Paint Ltd	PL08

Today's date is 22 March 20X1 and you are to enter these invoices into the analysed purchases day book given and total each of the columns

---

INVOICE

Mortimer & Co

Invoice to:
Julian Hargreaves
28 Flynn Avenue
Corton
TN16 4SJ

Pearl Park Estate
Tonbridge
TN14 6LM
Tel: 01883 461207
Fax: 01883 461208

Deliver to:
As above

Invoice no:	047992
Tax point:	20 March 20X1
VAT reg no:	641 3299 07

Code	Description	Quantity	VAT rate %	Unit price £	Amount exclusive of VAT £
LP4882	Lining Paper Grade 2	40 rolls	17 5%	2 80	112 00
GL117	Wallpaper Glue	4 tins (2 litres)	17 5%	10 65	42 60
					154 60

VAT at 17 5%	26 37
Total amount payable	180 97

Deduct discount of 2½% if paid within 14 days

INVOICE

Invoice to:
Julian Hargreaves
28 Flynn Avenue
Corton
TN16 4SJ

Deliver to:
As above

F L Decor Supplies

64/66 Main Road
Flimfield
TN22 4HT
Tel 01883 714206
Fax 01883 714321

Invoice no: 61624
Tax point: 18 March 20X1
VAT reg no   743 2116 05

Code	Description	Quantity	VAT rate %	Unit price £	Amount exclusive of VAT £
AG461	Anaglypta Wallpaper – White	16 rolls	17 5%	3 80	60 80

	60 80
Trade discount 10%	6 08
	54 72
VAT at 17 5%	9 57
Total amount payable	64 29

INVOICE

Invoice to:
Julian Hargreaves
28 Flynn Avenue
Corton
TN16 4SJ

Specialist Paint Ltd

Cedar House
Otford Way
Tonbridge
TN3 6AS
Tel 01883 445511
Fax: 01883 445512

Deliver to:
As above

Invoice no	05531
Tax point	20 March 20X1
VAT reg no:	666 4557 28

Code	Description	Quantity	VAT rate %	Unit price £	Amount exclusive of VAT £
PT4168	Eggshell Paint – Fuchsia	6 tins (2 litres)	17 5%	16 40	98 40
BS118	Horse Hair Paint Brush 50 mm	10	17 5%	8 85	88 50
					186 90

VAT at 17 5%   32 21

Total amount payable   219 11

Deduct discount of 1 5% if paid within 10 days

Purchases day book

Date	Invoice no	Code	Supplier	Total	VAT	Paint	Wallpaper	Other

Question 3

Nethan Builders have recently received the three credit notes given   They are to be recorded in the analysed purchases returns day book given

An extract from the purchase ledger coding manual shows:

Supplier	Purchase ledger code
Jenson Ltd	PL13
Haddow Bros	PL03
Magnum Supplies	PL16

Today's date is 3 May 20X1

You are to enter the credit notes into the analysed purchases returns day book and to total each of the columns

---

CREDIT NOTE

Jenson Ltd

Credit note to:
Nethan Builders
Brecon House
Stamford Road
Manchester
M16 4PL

30 Longfield Park
Kingsway
M45 2TP
Tel 0161 511 4666
Fax 0161 511 4777

Credit note no	CN06113
Tax point:	28 April 20X1
VAT reg no:	641 3229 45
Sales invoice no:	47792

Code	Description	Quantity	VAT rate %	Unit price £	Amount exclusive of VAT £
PL432115	Door Lining Set – Wood 32 × 115 mm	1	17 5%	30 25	30 25

	30 25
Trade discount 15%	4 54
	25 71
VAT at 17 5%	4 36
Total amount of credit	30 07

CREDIT NOTE

Credit note to:
Nethan Builders
Brecon House
Stamford Road
Manchester
M16 4PL

Haddow Bros
The White House
Standing Way
Manchester
M13 6FH
Tel 0161 560 3140
Fax: 0161 560 6140

Credit note no:	06132
Tax point:	27 April 20X1
VAT reg no:	460 3559 71

Code	Description	Quantity	VAT rate %	Unit price £	Amount exclusive of VAT £
PLY8FE1	Plywood Hardwood 2440 × 1220 mm	2	17 5%	17 80	35 60
					35 60
VAT at 17 5%					6 10
Total amount of credit					41 70

CREDIT NOTE

Credit note to:
Nethan Builders
Brecon House
Stamford Road
Manchester
M16 4PL

MAGNUM SUPPLIES

140/150 Park Estate
Manchester
M20 6EG
Tel 0161 561 3202
Fax: 0161 561 3200

Credit note no: C4163
Tax point   30 April 20X1
VAT reg no: 611 4337 90

Code	Description	Quantity	VAT rate %	Unit price £	Amount exclusive of VAT £
BU1628	Ventilator Brick	5	17 5%	9 20	46 00
					46 00
Trade discount 15%					6 90
					39 10
VAT at 17 5%					6 70
Total amount of credit					45 80

Purchases returns day book								
Date	Credit note no	Code	Supplier	Total	VAT	Wood	Bricks/ Cement	Consumables

Question 4

Curtain Decor is a business that makes curtains and blinds to order Its purchases are analysed between fabric purchases, header tape purchases and others A separate purchases returns day book is not kept so any credit notes received are recorded in the purchases day book The business only has five credit suppliers and they are as follows:

Mainstream Fabrics	PL01
C R Thorne	PL02
Fabric Supplies Ltd	PL03
Lillian Fisher	PL04
Headstream & Co	PL05

Today's date is 12 April 20X1 and given below are three invoices and a credit note These are to be entered into the analysed purchases day book and each column is to be totalled

INVOICE

Fabric Supplies Ltd

Invoice to:
Curtain Decor
Field House
Warren Lane
Hawkhurst TN23 1AT

12/14 Tike Road
Wadfield
TN11 4ZP
Tel 01882 467111
Fax: 01882 467112

Deliver to:
As above

Invoice no	06738
Tax point:	7 April 20X1
VAT reg no:	532 6741 09

Code	Description	Quantity	VAT rate %	Unit price £	Amount exclusive of VAT £
B116–14	Header Tape 14 cm	30 m	17 5%	4 62	138 60
P480–G	Fabric - Green	56 m	17 5%	14 25	798 00
					936 60
VAT at 17 5%					160 62
Total amount payable					1,097 22

Deduct discount of 2% if paid within 10 days

INVOICE

LILLIAN FISHER

Invoice to:
Curtain Decor
Field House
Warren Lane
Hawkhurst   TN23 1AT

Deliver to:
As above

61 Park Crescent
Hawkhurst
TN23 8GF
Tel: 01868 463501
Fax 01868 463502

Invoice no:	0328
Tax point	6 April 20X1
VAT reg no	469 7153 20

Code	Description	Quantity	VAT rate %	Unit price £	Amount exclusive of VAT £
TB06	Tie Back Cord - Yellow	10 m	17 5%	6 55	65 50
TB09	Tie Back Cord – Green	4 m	17 5%	6 55	26 20
					91 70

VAT at 17 5%

16 04

Total amount payable

107.74

CREDIT NOTE

Credit note to:
Curtain Decor
Field House
Warren Lane
Hawkhurst   TN23 1AT

Headstream & Co
140 Myrtle Place
Fenham
TN16 4SJ
Tel 01842 303136
Fax 01842 303137

Credit note no	CN0477
Tax point	7 April 20X1
VAT reg no	663 4892 77

Code	Description	Quantity	VAT rate %	Unit price £	Amount exclusive of VAT £
HT479	Header Tape 11 cm	2 m	17 5%	8 30	16 60
CCF614Y	CC Fabric - Yellow	4 m	17 5%	12 85	51 40
					68 00
VAT at 17 5%					11 90
Total credit					79 90

INVOICE

Invoice to:
Curtain Decor
Field House
Warren Lane
Hawkhurst   TN23 1AT

Mainstream Fabrics

Tree Tops House
Farm Road
Tonbridge
TN2 4XT
Tel: 01883 214121
Fax 01883 214122

Deliver to:
As above

Invoice no	07359
Tax point:	8 April 20X1
VAT reg no:	379 4612 04

Code	Description	Quantity	VAT rate %	Unit price £	Amount exclusive of VAT £
DG4167F	Design Guild Fabric - Fuchsia	23 m	17 5%	13 60	312 80
					312 80
Trade discount 10%					31 28
					281 52
VAT at 17 5%					48 52
Total amount payable					330 04

Deduct discount of 1½% if paid within 14 days

Purchases day book

Date	Invoice no	Code	Supplier	Total	VAT	Fabric	Header Tape	Other

Credit purchases: accounting (covering Chapter 13)

Question 1

Given below is the purchases day book for a business.

Purchases day book

Date	Invoice no	Code	Supplier	Total £	VAT £	Net £
20X1						
1 May	36558	PL03	L Jameson	393.91	58.66	335.25
1 May	102785	PL07	K Davison	124.96	18.61	106.35
3 May	92544	PL02	H Samuels	109.79	16.35	93.44
4 May	03542	PL04	G Rails	180.93	26.94	153.99
5 May	002633	PL01	T Ives	192.98	28 74	164.24
				1,002.57	149 30	853.27

You are required to:

♦   post the totals of the purchases day book to the main ledger accounts given.

♦   post the individual invoices to the creditors' accounts in the subsidiary ledger given.

Main ledger

Creditors control account

	£				£
		1 May	Balance b/d		3,104.67

VAT account

	£				£
		1 May	Balance b/d		723.56

Purchases account

		£			£
1 May	Balance b/d	24,367.48			

Subsidiary ledger

T Ives   PL01

	£				£
		1 May	Balance b/d		332.56

H Samuels   PL02

	£				£
		1 May	Balance b/d		286.90

L Jameson   PL03

	£				£
		1 May	Balance b/d		623.89

G Rails   PL04

	£				£
		1 May	Balance b/d		68.97

K Davison   PL07

	£				£
		1 May	Balance b/d		125 47

Question 2

Below you are given the purchases day book for a business for the week ending 24 February 20X1. You are required to:

♦ post the totals to the main ledger accounts given;

♦ post the individual entries to the subsidiary ledger accounts given.

Purchases day book

Date	Invoice no	Code	Supplier	Total	VAT	01	02	03	04
20/2/X1	46118	PL11	Fred Janitor	218 70	32 57	84 93		101 20	
	46119	PL07	S Doorman	189 53	28 22		86 51	74 80	
21/2/X1	46120	PL03	P & F Davis & Co	166 54	24 80	68 92	23 30		49 52
22/2/X1	CN462	PL11	Fred Janitor	(30 99)	(4 61)	(10 20)		(16 18)	
	46121	PL06	Clooney & Partner	230 58	34 34		87 54	60 08	48 62
23/2/X1	CN463	PL07	S Doorman	(21 51)	(3 20)		(18 31)		
24/2/X1	46122	PL03	P & F Davis & Co	189 23	28 18	78 40		82 65	
				942 08	140 30	222 05	179 04	302 55	98 14

Main ledger

Creditors control account

	£			£
		17/2	Balance b/d	2,357.57

VAT account

	£			£
		17/2	Balance b/d	662.47

Purchases – 01 account

		£			£
17/2	Balance b/d	14,275.09			

Purchases – 02 account

		£			£
17/2	Balance b/d	12,574.26			

Purchases - 03 account

		£			£
17/2	Balance b/d	29,384.74			

Purchases – 04 account

		£			£
17/2	Balance b/d	9,274.36			

Subsidiary ledger

P & F Davis & Co — PL03

		£			£
			17/2	Balance b/d	368.36

Clooney & Partner — PL06

		£			£
			17/2	Balance b/d	226.48

S Doorman — PL07

		£			£
			17/2	Balance b/d	218 47

Fred Janitor — PL11

		£			£
			17/2	Balance b/d	111.45

Question 3

Given below is the purchases day book for a business for the week ending 12 March 20X1.

You are required to:

♦ prepare the journal entry for the posting of the totals to the main ledger – the last journal number was 0253;

♦ post the individual entries to the subsidiary ledger accounts given.

Purchases day book

Date	Invoice no	Code	Supplier	Total	VAT	01	02	03	04
08/3/X1	06121	PL12	Homer Ltd	223 87	33 34	68 90			121 63
	11675	PL07	Forker & Co	207 24	30 86		70 20	106 18	
09/3/X1	46251	PL08	Print Associates	230 04	34 26			64 88	130 90
10/3/X1	016127	PL02	ABG Ltd	292 58	43 57	118 60	130 41		
	C4366	PL07	Forker & Co	(23 73)	(3 53)		(20 20)		
11/3/X1	77918	PL19	G Greg	169 69	25 27	69 82		74 60	
	06132	PL12	Homer Ltd	189 33	28 19	70 24			90 90
12/3/X1	CN477	PL02	ABG Ltd	(48 31)	(7 19)	(16 80)	(24 32)		
				1,240 71	184 77	310 76	156 09	245 66	343 43

JOURNAL ENTRY	No:
Prepared by:	
Authorised by:	
Date:	
Narrative:	

Account	Debit	Credit
TOTALS		

Subsidiary ledger

ABG Ltd   PL02

	£				£
		5/3	Balance b/d		486.90

Forker & Co   PL07

	£				£
		5/3	Balance b/d		503.78

Print Associates   PL08

	£				£
		5/3	Balance b/d		229.56

Homer Ltd   PL12

	£				£
		5/3	Balance b/d		734.90

G Greg   PL19

	£				£
		5/3	Balance b/d		67.89

Question 4

Given below is a purchases returns day book.

You are required to:

♦ post the totals to the main ledger accounts;

♦ post the individual entries to the subsidiary ledger accounts.

Purchases returns day book

Date	Credit note	Code	Supplier	Total	VAT	01	02	03	04
15/4/X1	C0179	PL16	J D Withers	27 49	4 09		23 40		
18/4/X1	C4772	PL06	F Williams	164 50	24 50	32 00		108 00	
19/4/X1	06638	PL13	K Bartlett	53 11	7 91	28 40			16 80
				245 10	36 50	60 40	23 40	108 00	16 80

Main ledger

Creditors control account

	£			£
		12/4	Balance b/f	12,678.57

VAT account

	£			£
		12/4	Balance b/f	1,023.90

Purchases returns – 01 account

	£			£
		12/4	Balance b/f	337.60

Purchases returns - 02 account

	£			£
		12/4	Balance b/f	228.59

Purchases returns - 03 account

	£			£
		12/4	Balance b/f	889.46

Purchases returns - 04 account

	£			£
		12/4	Balance b/f	362.78

Subsidiary ledger

F Williams				PL06
	£			£
		12/4	Balance b/f	673.47

K Bartlett				PL13
	£			£
		12/4	Balance b/f	421.36

J D Withers				PL16
	£			£
		12/4	Balance b/f	446 37

Making payments (covering Chapters 14 and 15)

Question 1

Given below are four invoices received by Nethan Builders that are to be paid today, 18 May 20X1 It is the business policy to take advantage of any settlement discounts possible If the cheques are written out today then they will reach the supplier on 20 May

You are required to complete a remittance advice and cheque, ready for signature by the owner, for each payment

---

INVOICE

Building Contract Supplies

Invoice to: Nethan Builders Brecon House Stamford Road Manchester M16 4PL	Unit 15 Royal Estate Manchester M13 2EF Tel: 0161 562 3041 Fax: 0161 562 3042
Deliver to: As above	Invoice no: 07742 Tax point: 8 May 20X1 VAT reg no: 776 4983 06

Code	Description	Quantity	VAT rate %	Unit price £	Amount exclusive of VAT £
SDGSL6	SDGS Softwood 47 × 225 mm	20 5 m	17 5%	8 30	170 15
					170 15

VAT at 17 5%

29 32

Total amount payable

199 47

Deduct discount of 1½% if paid within 14 days

INVOICE

Invoice to:
Nethan Builders
Brecon House
Stamford Road
Manchester
M16 4PL

Deliver to:
As above

Jenson Ltd
30 Longfield Park
Kingsway
M45 2TP
Tel 0161 511 4666
Fax: 0161 511 4777

Invoice no	47811
Tax point:	5 May 20X1
VAT reg no:	641 3229 45
Purchase order no:	7174

Code	Description	Quantity	VAT rate %	Unit price £	Amount exclusive of VAT £
PL432115	Door Lining Set 32 × 115 mm	6	17 5%	30 25	181 50

	181 50
Trade discount 15%	27 22
	154 28
VAT at 17 5%	26 18
Total amount payable	180 46

Deduct discount of 3% if paid within 14 days

INVOICE

MAGNUM SUPPLIES

Invoice to:
Nethan Builders
Brecon House
Stamford Road
Manchester
M16 4PL

Deliver to:
As above

140/150 Park Estate
Manchester
M20 6EG
Tel 0161 501 3202
Fax: 0161 501 3200

Invoice no:	077422
Tax point:	11 May 20X1
VAT reg no:	611 4337 90

Code	Description	Quantity	VAT rate %	Unit price £	Amount exclusive of VAT £
BH47732	House Bricks - Red	600	17 5%	1 24	744 00

	744 00
Trade discount 15%	111 60
	632 40
VAT at 17 5%	108 45
Total amount payable	740.85

Deduct discount of 2% if paid within 10 days

INVOICE

Haddow Bros

Invoice to:
Nethan Builders
Brecon House
Stamford Road
Manchester
M16 4PL

The White House
Standing Way
Manchester
M13 6FH
Tel: 0161 560 3140
Fax: 0161 560 6140

Deliver to:
As above

Invoice no:	G33940
Tax point:	9 May 20X1
VAT reg no	460 3559 71

Code	Description	Quantity	VAT rate %	Unit price £	Amount exclusive of VAT £
PLY8FE1	Plywood Hardwood 2440 × 1220 mm	24	17 5%	17 80	427 20
					427 20

VAT at 17 5%   73 26

Total amount payable   500 46

Deduct discount of 2% if paid within 10 days

REMITTANCE ADVICE

To:

Nethan Builders
Brecon House
Stamford Road
Manchester
M16 4PL

Tel:	0161 521 6411
Fax:	0161 530 6412
VAT Reg no:	471 3860 42
Date:	

Date	Invoice no	Amount £	Discount taken £	Paid £

	Total paid	£
	Cheque no	_____

REMITTANCE ADVICE

To:

Nethan Builders
Brecon House
Stamford Road
Manchester
M16 4PL

Tel: 0161 521 6411
Fax: 0161 521 6412
VAT Reg no: 471 3860 42
Date:

Date	Invoice no	Amount £	Discount taken £	Paid £

	Total paid	£
	Cheque no	_____

REMITTANCE ADVICE

To:

Nethan Builders
Brecon House
Stamford Road
Manchester
M16 4PL

Tel: 0161 521 6411
Fax: 0161 521 6412
VAT Reg no: 471 3860 42
Date:

Date	Invoice no	Amount £	Discount taken £	Paid £

	Total paid	£
	Cheque no	_____

REMITTANCE ADVICE

To:

Nethan Builders
Brecon House
Stamford Road
Manchester
M16 4PL

Tel:	0161 521 6411
Fax:	0161 521 6412
VAT Reg no:	471 3860 42
Date:	

Date	Invoice no	Amount £	Discount taken £	Paid £

	Total paid	£
	Cheque no	_____

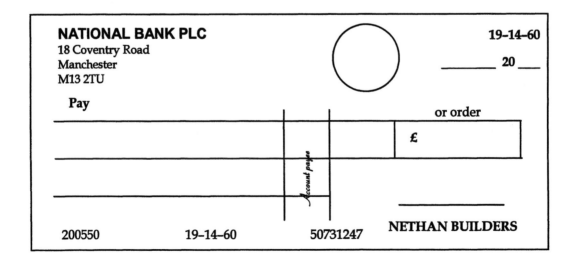

NATIONAL BANK PLC
18 Coventry Road
Manchester
M13 2TU

19–14–60

_____ 20 ___

Pay

or order

£

200550   19–14–60   50731247   NETHAN BUILDERS

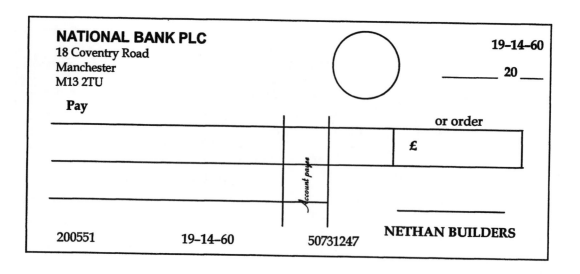

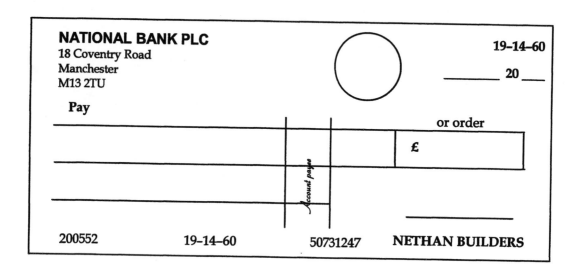

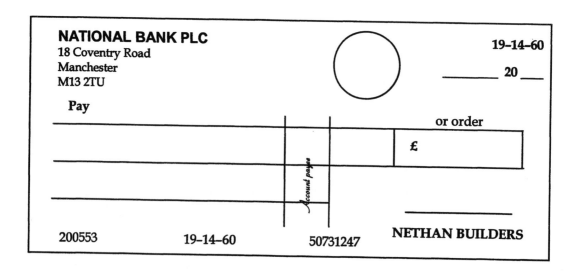

Accounting for payments (covering Chapter 16)

Question 1

Given below is the cheque listing for Nethan Builders for the week ended 30 May 20X1.

Cheque listing

Supplier	Code	Cheque number	Cheque amount £	Discount taken £
J M Bond	PL01	200572	247.56	
Magnum Supplies	PL16	200573	662.36	13.25
A J Broom Ltd	PL08	200574	153.57	
Jenson Ltd	PL13	200575	336.57	6.73
KKL Traders	PL20	200576	442.78	8.85
Cash purchases		200577	108.66	

The figure for cash purchases includes VAT at 17.5%.

You are required to:

♦ enter these amounts in the cash payments book provided and to total each of the columns;

♦ post the totals to the main ledger accounts given;

♦ post the individual entries to the subsidiary ledger accounts given.

Cash payments book

Date	Details	Cheque no	Code	Total £	VAT £	Creditors ledger £	Cash purchases £	Other £	Discounts received £

Main ledger

Creditors control account

	£			£
		23 May	Balance b/d	5,328.46

VAT account

	£			£
		23 May	Balance b/d	1,365.35

Purchases account

	£		£
23 May Balance b/d	36,785.90		

Discount received account

	£			£
		23 May	Balance b/d	1,573.56

Subsidiary ledger

J M Bond — PL01

	£			£
		23 May	Balance b/d	247.56

A J Broom Ltd — PL08

	£			£
		23 May	Balance b/d	524.36

Jenson Ltd — PL13

	£			£
		23 May	Balance b/d	512.36

Magnum Supplies — PL16

	£			£
		23 May	Balance b/d	675.61

KKL Traders — PL20

	£			£
		23 May	Balance b/d	612.46

Question 2

Given below is the cheque payment listing for a business for the week ending 8 May 20X1

Cheque payment listing				
Supplier	*Code*	*Cheque number*	*Cheque amount* £	*Discount taken* £
G Rails	PL04	001221	177.56	4.43
L Jameson	PL03	001222	257.68	7.73
Cash purchases		001223	216.43	
K Davison	PL07	001224	167.89	
T Ives	PL01	001225	289.06	5.79
Cash purchases		001226	263.78	
H Samuels	PL02	001227	124.36	

The cash purchases include VAT at the standard rate.

You are required to:

♦ enter the payments into the cash payments book given and total all of the columns;

♦ complete the journal for the posting of the totals to the main ledger – the last journal entry was number 1467;

♦ post the individual entries to the subsidiary ledger accounts given.

Cash payments book

Date	Details	Cheque no	Code	Total £	VAT £	Creditors ledger £	Cash purchases £	Other £	Discounts received £

JOURNAL ENTRY	No:		
Prepared by:			
Authorised by:			
Date:			
Narrative:			
Account		*Debit*	*Credit*
TOTALS			

Subsidiary ledger

T Ives PL01

	£				£
		1 May	Balance b/d		332.56

H Samuels PL02

	£				£
		1 May	Balance b/d		286.90

L Jameson PL03

	£				£
		1 May	Balance b/d		623.89

G Rails PL04

	£				£
		1 May	Balance b/d		181.99

K Davison PL07

	£				£
		1 May	Balance b/d		167.89

Question 3

Given below is the cheque listing for a business for the week ending 12 March 20X1

Cheque payment listing				
Supplier	*Code*	*Cheque number*	*Cheque amount £*	*Discount taken £*
Homer Ltd	PL12	03648	168.70	5.06
Forker & Co	PL07	03649	179.45	5.38
Cash purchases		03650	334.87	
Print Associates	PL08	03651	190.45	
ABG Ltd	PL02	03652	220.67	6.62
Cash purchases		03653	193.87	
G Greg	PL19	03654	67.89	

You are required to:

♦ enter the payments into the cash payments book and total each of the columns;

♦ post the totals to the main ledger accounts given;

♦ post the individual entries to the subsidiary ledger accounts given.

Cash payments book

Date	Details	Cheque no	Code	Total £	VAT £	Creditors ledger £	Cash purchases £	Other £	Discounts received £

Main ledger

Creditors control account

	£				£
		5/3	Balance b/d		4,136.24

VAT account

	£				£
		5/3	Balance b/d		1,372.56

Purchases account

		£		£
5/3	Balance b/d	20,465.88		

Discounts received account

	£				£
		5/3	Balance b/d		784.56

Subsidiary ledger

ABG Ltd   PL02

	£				£
		5/3	Balance b/d		486.90

Forker & Co   PL07

	£				£
		5/3	Balance b/d		503.78

Print Associates   PL08

	£				£
		5/3	Balance b/d		229.56

Homer Ltd   PL12

	£				£
		5/3	Balance b/d		734.90

G Greg   PL19

	£				£
		5/3	Balance b/d		67.89

Petty cash systems (covering Chapter 17)

Question 1

A business runs an imprest system with an imprest amount of £120. The rules of the petty cash system are as follows:

♦ only amounts of less than £30 can be paid out of petty cash, any larger claims must be dealt with by filling out a cheque requisition form;

♦ all petty cash claims over £5 must be supported by a receipt or invoice;

♦ the exception to this is that rail fares can be reimbursed without a receipt provided that the petty cash voucher is authorised by the department head;

♦ all other valid petty cash vouchers can be authorised by you, the petty cashier;

♦ all petty cash vouchers that are authorised are given a sequential number.

You have on your desk 10 petty cash vouchers which have been completed and you must decide which can be paid and which cannot.

PETTY CASH VOUCHER				
Authorised by	*Claimed by* J Athersych	*No*		
Date	*Description*		*Amount*	
15/3/X1	Coffee		4	83
	Milk		1	42
	Biscuits		0	79
		Total	7	04

Receipt is attached.

PETTY CASH VOUCHER				
Authorised by	*Claimed by* J Athersych	*No*		
Date	*Description*		*Amount*	
15/3/X1	Envelopes		4	85
		Total	4	85

No receipt.

PETTY CASH VOUCHER

Authorised by Department Head	Claimed by F Rivers	No	
Date	Description	Amount	
16/3/X1	Rail fare	12	80
	Total	12	80

No receipt.

PETTY CASH VOUCHER

Authorised by	Claimed by M Patterson	No	
Date	Description	Amount	
16/3/X1	Computer discs	4	20
	Printer paper	2	40
	Total	6	60

No receipt.

PETTY CASH VOUCHER

Authorised by	Claimed by D R Ray	No	
Date	Description	Amount	
17/3/X1	Lunch – entertaining clients	42	80
	Total	42	80

Bill attached.

PETTY CASH VOUCHER			
Authorised by	*Claimed by* J Athersych	*No*	
Date	*Description*	*Amount*	
17/3/X1	Milk	1	42
	Tea bags	2	28
	Total	3	70

No receipt.

PETTY CASH VOUCHER			
Authorised by	*Claimed by* D R Ray	*No*	
Date	*Description*	*Amount*	
18/3/X1	Rail fare	12	50
	Total	12	50

No receipt.

PETTY CASH VOUCHER			
Authorised by	*Claimed by* M Patterson	*No*	
Date	*Description*	*Amount*	
18/3/X1	Special delivery postage	19	50
	Total	19	50

Receipt attached.

PETTY CASH VOUCHER				
Authorised by	*Claimed by* M T Noble		*No*	
Date	*Description*		*Amount*	
18/3/X1	Ink for printer		17	46
	Total		17	46

Receipt attached.

PETTY CASH VOUCHER				
Authorised by	*Claimed by* J Norman		*No*	
Date	*Description*		*Amount*	
18/3/X1	Rail fare		7	60
	Total		7	60

No receipt.

Question 2

A business runs its petty cash system on an imprest system with an imprest amount of £100 per week. During the week ended 30 April 20X1 the following petty cash vouchers were paid:

Voucher no	Amount £	Reason
002534	4.68	Coffee/milk
002535	13.26	Postage
002536	10.27	Stationery (including £1.53 VAT)
002537	15.00	Taxi fare (including £2.23 VAT)
002538	6.75	Postage
002539	7.40	Train fare
002540	3.86	Stationery (including £0.57 VAT)

You are required to:

♦   write up these vouchers in the petty cash book given;

♦   post the totals of the petty cash book to the main ledger accounts given.

Petty cash book

Receipts			Payments								
Date	Narrative	Total £	Date	Narrative	Voucher no	Total £	Postage £	Stationery £	Tea & coffee £	Travel £	VAT £

Main ledger accounts

Postage account

	£		£
23 April Balance b/d	231.67		

Stationery account

	£		£
23 April Balance b/d	334.78		

Tea and coffee account

	£		£
23 April Balance b/d	55.36		

Travel expenses account

	£		£
23 April Balance b/d	579.03		

VAT account

	£		£
		23 April Balance b/d	967.44

Question 3

Given below are the petty cash vouchers that have been paid during the week ending 12 January 20X1 out of a petty cash box run on an imprest system of £150 per week. At the end of each week a cheque requisition is drawn up for a cheque for cash to bring the petty cash box back to the imprest amount.

Voucher no	Amount £	Reason
03526	13.68	Postage
03527	25.00	Staff welfare
03528	14.80	Stationery (including £2.20 VAT)
03529	12.00	Taxi fare (including £1.79 VAT)
03530	6.40	Staff welfare
03531	12.57	Postage
03532	6.80	Rail fare
03533	7.99	Stationery (including £1.19 VAT)
03534	18.80	Taxi fare (including £2.80 VAT)

You are required to:

♦ write up the petty cash book given;

♦ prepare the cheque requisition for the cash required to restore the petty cash box to the imprest amount;

♦ post the petty cash book totals to the main ledger accounts given.

Petty cash book											
Receipts			**Payments**								
Date	Narrative	Total £	Date	Narrative	Voucher no	Total £	Postage £	Staff welfare £	Stationery £	Travel expenses £	VAT £

```
┌─────────────────────────────────────────────────────────┐
│                                                           │
│  CHEQUE REQUISITION FORM                                  │
│                                                           │
│  CHEQUE DETAILS                                           │
│                                                           │
│  Date              .......................................│
│                                                           │
│  Payee             .......................................│
│                                                           │
│  Amount   £        .......................................│
│                                                           │
│  Reason ..................................................│
│                                                           │
│  Invoice no. (attached/to follow)  ......................│
│                                                           │
│  Receipt (attached/to follow)    ........................│
│                                                           │
│  Required by    (Print)      ......... ..................│
│                                                           │
│                 (Signature) .............................│
│                                                           │
│  Authorised by: ................. .......................│
│                                                           │
└─────────────────────────────────────────────────────────┘
```

Main ledger accounts

Postage account

		£		£
5 Jan	Balance b/d	248.68		

Staff welfare account

		£		£
5 Jan	Balance b/d	225.47		

Stationery account

		£		£
5 Jan	Balance b/d	176.57		

Travel expenses account

		£		£
5 Jan	Balance b/d	160.90		

VAT account

		£			£
			5 Jan	Balance b/d	2,385.78

Question 4

A business runs its petty cash on an imprest system with an imprest amount of £100 per week.

At the end of the week ending 22 May 20X1 the vouchers in the petty cash box were:

Voucher no	£
02634	13.73
02635	8.91
02636	10.57
02637	3.21
02638	11.30
02639	14.66

The cash remaining in the petty cash box was made up as follows:

£10 note	1
£5 note	2
£2 coin	3
£1 coin	7
50p coin	5
20p coin	4
10p coin	1
5p coin	2
2p coin	3
1p coin	6

You are required to reconcile the petty cash in the box to the vouchers in the box at 22 May 20X1 and if it does not reconcile to suggest reasons for the difference.

Payroll procedures (covering Chapter 18)

Question 1

An employee has gross pay for a week of £368.70. The PAYE for the week is £46.45, the employer's NIC £30.97 and the employee's NIC £23.96.

What is the employee's net pay for the week?

Question 2

Given below is the wages book for the month of May 20X1 for a small business with four employees.

Wages book

Employee number	Gross pay £	PAYE £	Employee's NIC £	Employer's NIC £	Net pay £
001	1,200	151	78	101	971
002	1,400	176	91	118	1,133
003	900	113	58	76	729
004	1,550	195	101	130	1,254
	5,050	635	328	425	4,087

You are required to use the totals from the wages book for the month to write up the wages ledger accounts given below.

Gross wages control account

	£		£

Wages expense account

	£		£
30 April Balance b/d	23,446		

Inland Revenue account

	£		£
19 May CPB	760	30 April Balance b/d	760

PRACTICE DEVOLVED ASSESSMENT 1

JP HARTNELL LTD

Performance criteria covered

Element 2.1 Process documents relating to goods and services received

◆ Suppliers' invoices and credit notes are checked against delivery notes, ordering documentation and evidence that goods or services have been received

◆ Totals and balances are correctly calculated and checked on suppliers' invoices

◆ Documents are correctly entered as primary records according to organisational procedures

◆ Entries are coded and recorded in the appropriate ledger

◆ Discrepancies are identified and either resolved or referred to the appropriate person if outside own authority

Range

Documents

◆ suppliers' invoices

◆ purchase orders

◆ goods received notes

◆ credit notes

Primary records

◆ purchases day book

◆ purchases returns day book

Discounts

◆ trade

◆ settlement

DATA AND TASKS

The situation and the tasks to be completed are set out on the following pages.

The simulation is divided into **twelve tasks.**

This assessment also contains a large amount of data which you may need to complete the tasks. You are advised to read the whole of the assessment before commencing as all of the information may be of value and is not necessarily supplied in the sequence in which you might wish to deal with it.

A high level of accuracy is required. Check your work carefully before handing it in.

Correcting fluid may be used but it should be used in moderation. Errors should be crossed out neatly and clearly. You should write in black ink, not pencil

Documents provided

Documents received from suppliers	-	Invoices Credit notes
Completed copies of internal documents	-	Purchase orders Goods received notes
Blank copies of internal forms	-	Purchases day book Purchases returns day book
Other internal information	-	Main codes (extract) Supplier codes

THE SITUATION

Business name	J P Hartnell Ltd
Location	Four manufacturing sites in Warrington, Consett, Hastings and Solihull
	Head office in Milton Keynes
Business	Manufacture and distribution of doors

Business profile

Each of the four manufacturing sites is responsible for its own purchases of goods and services from suppliers (including heat, light and power).

Purchase invoices received are processed locally, then details are sent to head office. All supplier records are maintained centrally. All account queries and statements of account are dealt with centrally.

Solihull site

The Solihull site manufactures the company's full range of doors then distributes them with its fleet of lorries.

Personnel

Operations manager	Neil McCann
Finance manager	Paul Snow
Accounts assistant	You

Your responsibilities include checking and recording purchase invoices.

Company's procedures re invoices

1   All invoices and credit notes are stamped and coded on receipt.

2   Invoices and credit notes are passed to you to check the accuracy of the calculations (clerical accuracy).

3   Invoices are checked against **purchase orders and goods received notes.**

4   Any discrepancies are noted on the face of the purchase invoice or credit note.

5   Invoices and credit notes are recorded at their original value in a **purchase day book** and **purchases returns day book** regardless of any errors.

6   The purchase day book, purchases returns day book, credit notes and invoices are passed to Paul Snow for approval.

7   A listing of the purchase day book and purchases returns day book is sent to head office. The invoices and credit notes are kept at the Solihull site and are later used to prepare cheque payments.

Terms of trade

Certain of the company's suppliers offer settlement discounts.

The company is registered for VAT.

THE TASKS TO BE COMPLETED

Today is 11 September 20X1.

You are required to process and record a batch of purchase invoices. You must follow the company's procedures as described above.

TASK 1   Check the accuracy of the calculations on the invoices and check the invoices against the purchase orders and goods received notes. Prepare a schedule of errors.

TASK 2   Record the invoices at their **original value** in the purchase day book, regardless of any errors.

TASK 3   Note any discrepancies on the face of the purchase invoice.

TASK 4   All purchase invoices must be recorded even if they are inaccurate.

             Why is this procedure used?

TASK 5   What should happen to invoices which are

             (a)   clerically inaccurate or have the wrong VAT charge?

             (b)   duplicates?

             (c)   for goods which have not been delivered?

TASK 6   Three of the GRNs held by you have not been matched to purchase invoices.

             What action should you take?

TASK 7   Post the totals of the purchases day book to the main ledger accounts given.

TASK 8   Enter each invoice into the individual creditors' account in the subsidiary ledger given.

TASK 9   You now have three credit notes which you must check for accuracy.

TASK 10   Enter the credit notes in the purchases returns day book given.

TASK 11   Post the totals of the purchases returns day book to the main ledger accounts.

TASK 12   Post the individual entries in the purchases returns day book to the creditors' accounts in the subsidiary ledger.

Sales invoice no 35702

Smith Fittings Ltd

Head office: 47 Acre Way, Northway Industrial Estate, Solihull B90 4BM

Telephone 0121 402 5578

Tax point 3 September 20X1

VAT registration no 236 1883 45

Supply by sale to:

JP Hartnell Ltd
Thelwell Road
Northway Industrial Estate
Solihull
B90 0AY

CENTRAL MANAGEMENT	
N/L CODE	905
APPROVED	

5 lever mortice security lock 3 inch (brass)

    50 @ £34.78 each   £1,739.00

VAT at 17.5%   £304.33

                                                      £2,043.33

Please send your remittance to the above address

Sales invoice no 35698

Smith Fittings Ltd

Head office: 47 Acre Way, Northway Industrial Estate, Solihull B90 4BM

Telephone 0121 402 5578

Tax point 1 September 20X1

VAT registration no 236 1883 45

Supply by sale to:

```
JP Hartnell Ltd
Thelwell Road
Northway Industrial Estate
Solihull
B90 0AY
```

CENTRAL MANAGEMENT	
N/L CODE	905
APPROVED	

```
5 lever mortice security lock 3 inch

50 @ £14.60 each                                          £730.00

VAT at 17.5%                                              £127.75
                                                         _____

                                                          £857.75
                                                         _____
```

Please send your remittance to the above address

Sales invoice no 35745

Smith Fittings Ltd

Head office: 47 Acre Way, Northway Industrial Estate, Solihull B90 4BM

Telephone 0121 402 5578

Tax point 4 September 20X1

VAT registration no 236 1883 45

Supply by sale to:

JP Hartnell Ltd

Thelwell Road

Northway Industrial Estate

Solihull

B90 0AY

CENTRAL MANAGEMENT	
N/L CODE	905
APPROVED	

7 lever mortice security lock

10 @ £19.46 each	£194.60
VAT at 17.5%	£34.06
	£228.66

Please send your remittance to the above address

SALES INVOICE

E L Stanley & Co   36479

Address
Unit 57
Prince Charles Way
Jubilee Industrial Estate   Telephone   0121 583 2233
Solihull B90 5OJ   Fax   0121 582 3758

Tax point 31/8/20X1   **VAT Reg No**   **567 8844 27**

Sale

J P Hartnell Ltd
Thelwell Works
Thelwell Road
Solihull
B90 0AY

CENTRAL MANAGEMENT	
N/L CODE	903
APPROVED	

Customer code HART 45

Description	Unit price £	VAT rate %	Total excl VAT £	VAT £	
Brass butt hinges					
38mm × 20	1.21	17.5	24.20	4.235	
50mm × 30	1.62	17.5	48.60	8.505	
			72.80	12.74	
		VAT	12.74		
			85.54	:	£85.54

SALES INVOICE

E L Stanley & Co   36534

Address
Unit 57
Prince Charles Way
Jubilee Industrial Estate   Telephone   0121 583 2233
Solihull B90 5OJ   Fax   0121 582 3758

Tax point 2/9/20X1   **VAT Reg No**   567 8844 27

Sale

J P Hartnell Ltd
Thelwell Works
Thelwell Road
Solihull
B90 0AY

CENTRAL MANAGEMENT	
N/L CODE	903
APPROVED	

Customer code HART 45

Description	Unit price £	VAT rate %	Total excl VAT £	VAT £
Brass butt hinges				
75mm × 20	2.20	17.5	44.00	7.70
100mm × 10	5.10	17.5	51.00	8.925
			95.00	16.625
		VAT	16.63	
			111.63	:£111.63

Timber Supply Company Ltd

SALES INVOICE   2373 AX

Address
283 Winding Lane
Sale
Manchester
M18 6GJ

Customer
J P Hartnell Ltd   **H056**
Thelwell Works
Thelwell Road
Solihull
West Midlands B90 0AY

VAT registration no   245 1118 95

Tax point   10 September 20X1

Sale

DESCRIPTION	UNIT PRICE £	VAT RATE %	TOTAL £
100	sheets		
1220 × 2440 mm × 15 mm supergrade	40.30	17.5	4,030.00
VAT payable			694.67
			4,724.67

CENTRAL MANAGEMENT	
N/L CODE	902
APPROVED	

Terms of trade

1 5% discount on invoices paid within 14 days

....

Remittance advice

Customer   J P Hartnell Ltd (H056)
Invoice no   2373 AX
Remittance   £4,724.67

Please send to the address above

Timber Supply Company Ltd

SALES INVOICE   2567 BX

Address   **Customer**
283 Winding Lane   J P Hartnell Ltd   **H056**
Sale   Thelwell Works
Manchester   Thelwell Road
M18 6GJ   Solihull
                                                       West Midlands B90 0AY

VAT registration no   245 1118 95

Tax point   10 September 20X1

Sale

DESCRIPTION	UNIT PRICE £	VAT RATE %	TOTAL £
100	sheets		
1220 × 2440 mm × 15 mm supergrade	40.30	17.5	4,030.00
VAT payable			694.67
			4,724.67

CENTRAL MANAGEMENT	
N/L CODE	902
APPROVED	

Terms of trade

1.5% discount on invoices paid within 14 days

....

Remittance advice

Customer   J P Hartnell Ltd (H056)
Invoice no   2567 BX
Remittance   £4,724.67

Please send to the address above

Sales invoice 36598

Tipp & Sons Ltd

Fountain House, Avalon Way, Solihull B90 7TY
Telephone 0121 345 7284

Tax point 6/9/20X1   **VAT Reg No**   873 8555 92

Supply by sale

J P Hartnell Ltd
Thelwell Works
Thelwell Road
Solihull B90 0AY

Description	Unit price £	VAT rate %	Total excl VAT £	VAT £
Stainless steel screws				
35mm × 4 kg	7.29	17.5	29.16	13.81
45mm × 6 kg	11.86	17.5	71.16	12.45
			100.32	26.26
		VAT	26.26	
			126.58	: £126.58

Please send your remittance to:
Fountain House, Avalon Way, Solihull, B90 7TY

Younge Timber Company Ltd

Sales invoice 289349

Younge House
478 Fentham Road
SOLIHULL
B90 8NM

Tax point 7 September 20X1

| *Telephone* | *0121 678 1948* |
| *Fax* | *0121 678 2865* |

VAT Reg No 228 9843 04

Sale to:
J P Hartnell Ltd
Thelwell Works
Thelwell Road
Solihull
B90 0AY

Description	*Unit price* £	*Total* £
Blockwood interior		
100 sheets		
2440 mm × 1220 mm (21 mm)	24.98	2,498.00
Value Added Tax at 17.5%		428.41
		2,926.41

CENTRAL MANAGEMENT	
N/L CODE	902
APPROVED	

Trade terms

2% discount 21 days

REMITTANCE ADVICE

J P Hartnell Ltd
Thelwell Works
Thelwell Road
Solihull B90 0AY

Invoice 289349

Remittance £2,926.41
Discount

PURCHASE ORDER   **Order no** 22928

J P HARTNELL LTD

Thelwell Works Thelwell Road Solihull B90 0AY
Tel 0121 556 3388 Fax 0121 557 9877

To: E L Stanley & Co   Date 27/8/20X1
     Unit 57
     Prince Charles Way
     Jubilee Industrial Estate
     Solihull
     B90 5OJ

Please supply and deliver the following goods to the above address

Delivery within 7 days carriage paid

Quantity	Product code	Description	Price (excl VAT) £ p
10		100mm brass butt hinges	51.00
20		75mm brass butt hinges	44.00

N McCann

Neil McCann
Operations Manager

VAT reg no 334 0988 11

PURCHASE ORDER

Order no 22933

J P HARTNELL LTD

Thelwell Works Thelwell Road Solihull B90 0AY
Tel 0121 556 3388 Fax 0121 557 9877

To: Smith Fittings Ltd
      47 Acre Way
      Northway Industrial Estate
      Solihull
      B90 4BM

Date 29/8/20X1

Please supply and deliver the following goods to the above address

Delivery within 7 days carriage paid

Quantity	Product code	Description	Price (excl VAT) £ p
10	344	7 lever mortice security lock	194.60
50	369	5 lever mortice security lock 3 inch (brass)	1,739.00

N McCann

Neil McCann
Operations Manager

VAT reg no 334 0988 11

PURCHASE ORDER   **Order no.** 22937

J P HARTNELL LTD

Thelwell Works Thelwell Road Solihull B90 0AY
Tel 0121 556 3388 Fax 0121 557 9877

To: Tipp & Sons Ltd   Date 31/8/20X1
     Fountain House
     Avalon Way
     Solihull
     B90 7TY

Please supply and deliver the following goods to the above address

Delivery within 7 days carriage paid

Quantity	Product code	Description	Price (excl VAT) £ p
6 kg		45mm stainless steel screws	71.16
4 kg		35mm stainless steel screws	29.16
5 kg		35mm brass screws (special)	78.90
3 kg		50mm brass screws (special)	55.86

N McCann

Neil McCann
Operations Manager

VAT reg no 334 0988 11

PURCHASE ORDER **Order no.** 22940

J P HARTNELL LTD

Thelwell Works Thelwell Road Solihull B90 0AY
Tel 0121 556 3388 Fax 0121 557 9877

To: Timber Supply Company Ltd   Date 2/9/20X1
      283 Winding Lane
      Sale
      Manchester
      M18 6GJ

Please supply and deliver the following goods to the above address

Delivery within 7 days carriage paid

Quantity	Product code	Description	Price (excl VAT) £ p
100 sheets	4656	1220 × 2440 mm × 15 mm supergrade	4,030.00

N McCann

Neil McCann
Operations Manager

VAT reg no 334 0988 11

PURCHASE ORDER   **Order no.** 22941

J P HARTNELL LTD

Thelwell Works Thelwell Road Solihull B90 0AY
Tel 0121 556 3388 Fax 0121 557 9877

To: Younge Timber Company Ltd   Date 2/9/20X1
     Younge House
     478 Fentham Road
     Solihull
     B90 8NM

Please supply and deliver the following goods to the above address

Delivery within 7 days carriage paid

Quantity	Product code	Description	Price (excl VAT) £ p
100 sheets		2440 × 1220 × 21mm interior blockwood	2,498.00

N McCann

Neil McCann
Operations Manager

VAT reg no 334 0988 11

	Accounts copy

GOODS RECEIVED NOTE

Date 31/8/X1 **Received by** F Carter **GRN no 5550**

Site S/hull **Checked by** F Carter

Supplier	Details	Order no
E L Stanley	20 × 38mm 30 × 50mm brass butt hinges	22919

	Accounts copy

GOODS RECEIVED NOTE

Date 31/8/X1 **Received by** F Carter **GRN no 5551**

Site S/hull **Checked by** G Edwards

Supplier	Details	Order no
Smith Fittings	50 × 5 lever 3 inch mortice security lock	22926

Accounts copy

GOODS RECEIVED NOTE

| Date | 1/9/X1 | **Received by** | F Carter | **GRN no 5552** |
| **Site** | S/hull | **Checked by** | F Carter | |

Supplier	Details	Order no
E L Stanley	20 × 75mm 10 × 100mm brass butt hinges	22928

Accounts copy

GOODS RECEIVED NOTE

| Date | 1/9/X1 | **Received by** | F Carter | **GRN no 5553** |
| **Site** | S/hull | **Checked by** | F Carter | |

Supplier	Details	Order no
McDonald Trading	20 × Georgian door handles	22930

<table>
<tr><td colspan="3" align="right">Accounts copy</td></tr>
</table>

GOODS RECEIVED NOTE

Date   3/9/X1   **Received by**   F Carter   **GRN no 5554**

Site   S/hull   **Checked by**   F Carter

Supplier	Details	Order no
Smith Fittings	50 × 5 lever mortice security lock 3" (brass)	22933

<table>
<tr><td colspan="3" align="right">Accounts copy</td></tr>
</table>

GOODS RECEIVED NOTE

Date   4/9/X1   **Received by**   F Carter   **GRN no 5555**

Site   S/hull   **Checked by**   F Carter

Supplier	Details	Order no
A1 Products	10 × 5 lever mortice security lock	22934

		Accounts copy
	GOODS RECEIVED NOTE	

Date 5/9/ X1   **Received by**   F Carter   **GRN no 5556**

Site   S/hull   **Checked by**   G Edwards

Supplier	Details	Order no
Tipp & Sons	4 kg × 35mm 6 kg × 45mm stainless steel screws	22937

		Accounts copy
	GOODS RECEIVED NOTE	

Date 6/9/ X1   **Received by**   F Carter   **GRN no 5557**

Site   S/hull   **Checked by**   F Carter

Supplier	Details	Order no
Chantry Products	2 kg × 35mm brass screws	22939

Accounts copy

GOODS RECEIVED NOTE

Date 6/9/ X1 **Received by** F Carter **GRN no** 5558

Site S/hull **Checked by** F Carter

Supplier	Details	Order no
Younge Timber	100 sheets 2440 × 1220mm × 21mm interior blockwood	22941

Accounts copy

GOODS RECEIVED NOTE

Date 10/9/ X1 **Received by** F Carter **GRN no** 5559

Site S/hull **Checked by** F Carter

Supplier	Details	Order no
Timber Supply Co	100 sheets 1220 × 2440mm × 15mm supergrade	22940

PURCHASE DAY BOOK

Site _____   **Date** _____

Prepared by _____

Code	Supplier	Invoice no	Total		VAT		902		903		904		905	

Main ledger

Creditors control account

	£			£
		4 Sep	Balance b/d	37,589.07

VAT account

	£			£
		4 Sep	Balance b/d	7,374.46

Purchases - 902

		£		£
4 Sep	Balance b/d	100,357.36		

Purchases - 903

		£		£
4 Sep	Balance b/d	4,284.60		

Purchases - 904

		£		£
4 Sep	Balance b/d	3,847.19		

Purchases - 905

		£		£
4 Sep	Balance b/d	12,395.36		

Purchases returns - 902

	£			£
		4 Sep	Balance b/d	362.78

Purchases returns - 903

	£			£
		4 Sep	Balance b/d	1,304.89

Purchases returns - 904

	£			£
		4 Sep	Balance b/d	221.78

Purchases returns - 905

	£			£
		4 Sep	Balance b/d	1,587.63

Subsidiary ledger

A J Broom & Co110

	£			£
		4 Sep	Balance b/d	378.90

Smith Fittings120

	£			£
		4 Sep	Balance b/d	3,730.35

Tipp & Sons121

	£			£
		4 Sep	Balance b/d	315.37

Younge Timber122

	£			£
		4 Sep	Balance b/d	4,739.21

E L Stanley123

	£			£
		4 Sep	Balance b/d	264.78

Timber Supply124

	£			£
		4 Sep	Balance b/d	16,483.93

CREDIT NOTE

E L Stanley & Co

CN6337

Address
Unit 57
Prince Charles Way
Jubilee Industrial Estate   Telephone   0121 583 2233
Solihull B90 5OJ   Fax   0121 582 3758

Tax point 2/9/20X1   **VAT Reg No**   **567 8844 27**

Credit note

J P Hartnell Ltd
Thelwell Works
Thelwell Road
Solihull
B90 0AY

CENTRAL MANAGEMENT	
N/L CODE	903
APPROVED	

Sales invoice ref 36504

Customer code HART 45

Description	Unit price £	VAT rate %	Total excl VAT £	VAT £
Brass butt hinges				
100mm × 10	5.10	17.5	51.00	8.92
			51.00	
		VAT	8.92	
			59.92	:£59.92

CREDIT NOTE

A J Broom & Company Limited

Credit note to:
J P Hartnell Ltd
Thelwell Road
Northway Ind Estate
Solihull
B90 0AY

59 Parkway
Manchester
M2 6EG
Tel: 0161 560 3392
Fax 0161 560 5322

Credit note no: C4680
Tax point: 2 September 20X1
VAT reg no: 496 3221 84

Code	Description	Quantity	VAT rate %	Unit price £	Amount exclusive of VAT £
046771	Brass Hinge 50 mm	20	17 5%	1 80	36 00

Trade discount 10%

CENTRAL MANAGEMENT	
N/L CODE	903
APPROVED	

VAT at 17.5%

Total amount of credit

36.00
3 60
32.40
5 67
38 07

Credit note no 4116

Smith Fittings Ltd

Head office: 47 Acre Way, Northway Industrial Estate, Solihull B90 4BM

Telephone 0121 402 5578

Tax point 1 September 20X1

VAT registration no 236 1883 45

Credit note to:

JP Hartnell Ltd
Thelwell Road
Northway Industrial Estate
Solihull
B90 0AY

CENTRAL MANAGEMENT	
N/L CODE	905
APPROVED	

Sales invoice ref 35601

5 lever mortice security lock 3 inch

10 @ £14.60 each	£146.00
VAT at 17.5%	£25.55
	£171.55

Purchases Returns Day Book

Site: Date:

Prepared by:

Code	Supplier	Credit note no	Total	VAT	902	903	904	905

MAIN CODES (extract)

Purchases

902	Wood, wooden components
903	Hinges
904	Fixings, screws and nails
905	Locks

SUPPLIER CODES

101	Brown and Hargreaves Ltd
102	Joseph Walter and Associates
103	English Gas plc
104	P O'Ryan
105	MacDougal Engineering Ltd
106	Solihull Borough Council
107	J Walter
108	The General Purpose Stationery Company
109	English Telecomm
110	A J Broom & Company Ltd
111	West Midlands Water plc
112	McDonald Trading Company
113	Newman and Royston Ltd
114	Original Brass Fitting Company Ltd
115	H Freeman Timber Supplies
116	The Atlas Group plc
117	A1 Products
118	Hardy Supplies Ltd
119	7 Stars Trading Company
120	Smith Fittings Ltd
121	Tipp & Sons Ltd
122	Younge Timber Company Ltd
123	EL Stanley
124	Timber Supply Company Ltd
125	Parker and Fellows Supplies

PRACTICE DEVOLVED ASSESSMENT 2
NATURAL PRODUCTS LTD

Performance criteria covered

Element 2.1 Process documents relating to goods and services received

♦ Documents are correctly entered as primary records according to organisational procedures

♦ Entries are coded and recorded in the appropriate ledger

♦ Discrepancies are identified and either resolved or referred to the appropriate person if outside own authority

♦ Communications with suppliers regarding accounts are handled politely and effectively

Range

Primary records

♦ purchase day book
♦ purchase returns day book

DATA AND TASKS

The situation and the tasks to be completed are set out on the following pages.

The simulation is divided into six tasks.

This booklet also contains a large amount of data which you may need to complete the tasks. You are advised to read the whole of the simulation before commencing as all of the information may be of value and is not necessarily supplied in the sequence in which you might wish to deal with it.

A high level of accuracy is required. Check your work carefully before handing it in.

Correcting fluid may be used but it should be used in moderation. Errors should be crossed out neatly and clearly. You should write in black ink, not pencil.

Documents provided

Internal ledgers	-	Purchase day book
	-	Purchase returns day book
	-	Subsidiary (purchases) ledger accounts
	-	Main ledger (extracts)
	-	Journal (extract)
Other internal information	-	Invoice and credit note listings
	-	Main ledger listing (extract)
Document received from supplier	-	Statement

THE SITUATION

Business name	Natural Products Ltd	
Location	Taunton, Somerset	
Personnel	Managing director	Cindy Taylor
	Sales director	Jason Taylor
	Production director	Tracy Yard
	Financial director	Steve Roberts
Business	Manufacture, wholesale and mail order sale of toiletries and cosmetics	

Business profile

The business was started by Cindy Taylor, supplying natural products to retail chains and on mail order.

Accounts department

Accounts supervisor	Caroline Everley
Ledger clerk	You
Administration and payroll	Robert Foster
Cashier and petty cashier	Trudi Roberts

The company has grown very quickly in a short space of time All systems are manual although a computer feasibility study is currently being carried out.

Terms of trade

The company is registered for VAT. All sales are standard-rated.

Certain suppliers offer settlement discounts.

THE TASKS TO BE COMPLETED

Today is 5 February 20X1.

Robert Foster has provided you with the purchase invoice and credit note listing for the week ending 30 January 20X1.

TASK 1   Enter the purchase invoices in the purchase day book given. You will find the supplier codes with the main ledger listing.

TASK 2   Enter the credit notes in the purchases returns day book.

TASK 3   Post the individual transactions from the purchase day book and purchases returns day book to the appropriate accounts in the subsidiary (purchases) ledgers.

TASK 4   Write up the journal for the posting of the totals of the purchase day book. Post the totals from the purchase day book to the main ledger. The last journal was number 1312.

TASK 5   Write up the journal for the posting of the totals of the purchases returns day book and post these amounts to the main ledger.

(The entries for cash have already been made in the main and subsidiary (purchases) ledger accounts.)

TASK 6   Caroline Everley is very concerned about the statement of account sent by Dehlavi Kosmetatos as your records show that there is no balance owing to this supplier. Reconcile the statement to the ledger account and identify any discrepancies.

PURCHASE INVOICE LISTING
30/1/X1

Invoice no

111333	Bruning & Soler	£561.55 plus VAT – essential oils
111334	Dehlavi Kosmetatos	£402.29 plus VAT offering a 2% settlement discount – emulsifiers and preservatives
111335	James Ellington	£98.10 plus VAT – colours
111336	James Ellington	£499.10 plus VAT – essential oils £191.60 plus VAT - colours
111337	Greig Handling	£262.22 plus VAT – oils and waxes
111338	Hartley Chemicals	£479.41 plus VAT – oils and waxes
111339	Hartley Chemicals	£74.81 plus VAT – oils and waxes
111340	Mortimer, Hassell	£180.26 plus VAT – essential oils
111341	Mortimer, Hassell	£799.07 plus VAT – oils and waxes
111342	Natural Ingredients	£1,175.60 plus VAT – oils and waxes

---

CREDIT NOTE LISTING
30/1/X1

Credit note no

6273	Greig Handling	£29.95 plus VAT – oils and waxes
6274	Mortimer, Hassell	£68.70 plus VAT – essential oils

PURCHASE DAY BOOK

30/1/X1

Code	Supplier	Invoice no	Total		151		152		153		154		VAT	

PURCHASE RETURNS DAY BOOK

30/1/X1

Code	Supplier	Credit note no	Total		161		162		163		164		VAT	

SUBSIDIARY (PURCHASES) LEDGER ACCOUNTS

Supplier	Bruning & Soler Ltd			Account number		B103	
Address							
Telephone							
Date	Transaction	£		Date	Transaction	£	
8/1/X1	Cash	329	50	1/1/X1	b/f	329	50

Supplier	Dehlavi Kosmetatos			Account number		D101	
Address							
Telephone							
Date	Transaction	£		Date	Transaction	£	
3/1/X1	Cash	645	10	1/1/X1	b/f	656	30
	Discount	11	20				
30/1/X1	Cash	463	24				
	Discount	8	04				

SUBSIDIARY (PURCHASES) LEDGER ACCOUNTS

Supplier	Greig Handling (Import) Ltd			Account number		G103	
Address							
Telephone							
Date	Transaction	£		Date	Transaction	£	
8/1/X1	Cash	25	68	1/1/X1	b/f	25	68
				8/1/X1	Inv 110990	119	50

Supplier	Hartley Chemicals Ltd			Account number		H102	
Address							
Telephone							
Date	Transaction	£		Date	Transaction	£	
1/1/X1	b/f	55	60				

SUBSIDIARY (PURCHASES) LEDGER ACCOUNTS

Supplier	Mortimer, Hassell & Co			Account number		M102	

Address

Telephone

Date	Transaction	£		Date	Transaction	£	
				8/1/X1	Inv 110989	811	30

Supplier	Natural Ingredients Ltd			Account number		N101	

Address

Telephone

Date	Transaction	£		Date	Transaction	£	
30/1/X1	Cash	134	13	15/1/X1	Inv 110999	135	87
	Discount	1	74				

SUBSIDIARY (PURCHASES) LEDGER ACCOUNTS

Supplier	Rendell & Sayers			Account number		R102	
Address							
Telephone							
Date	Transaction	£		Date	Transaction	£	
8/1/X1	Cash	246	26	1/1/X1	b/f	248	41
	Discount	2	12				

Supplier	James Ellington			Account number		E103	
Address							
Telephone							
Date	Transaction	£		Date	Transaction	£	

MAIN LEDGER

Account name	Oils & Waxes		Account no 151	
Narrative	£		Narrative	£
23/1/X1 b/f	202,511	60		

Account name	Essential Oils		Account no 152	
Narrative	£		Narrative	£
23/1/X1 b/f	112,388	71		

Account name	Emulsifiers and Preservatives		Account no 153	
Narrative	£		Narrative	£
23/1/X1 b/f	50,115	90		

MAIN LEDGER

Account name	Colours			Account no	154	
Narrative	£		Narrative		£	
23/1/X1 b/f	23,905	20				

Account name		Trade creditors			Account no	020	
Narrative		£		Narrative		£	
3/1/X1	Cash 1-2	14,204	17	1/1/X1 b/f		28,958	33
	Discount 1-2	217	27				
8/1/X1	Cash 1-3	12,857	77	8/1/X1 Invoices 1-4		7,335	56
	Discount 1-3	80	53				
15/1/X1	Credit notes			15/1/X1 Invoices 1-6		6,201	38
	1-7	203	60				
30/1/X1	Cash 1-12	14,995	60	23/1/X1 Adjustment 1-8		711	60
	Discount	113	80				
	1-12						

Account name	VAT control account			Account no	022	
Narrative	£		Narrative		£	
			23/1/X1 b/f		5,311	90

Main ledger

Account name	Purchases returns – oils and waxes		Account no 161		
Narrative	£		Narrative	£	
			23/1/X1 b/f	6,395	48

Account name	Purchases returns – essential oils		Account no 162		
Narrative	£		Narrative	£	
			23/1/X1 b/f	3,125	24

Account name	Purchases returns – emulsifiers and preservatives		Account no 163		
Narrative	£		Narrative	£	
			23/1/X1 b/f	1,486	07

Account name	Purchases returns - colours		Account no	164	
Narrative	£		Narrative	£	
			23/1/X1 b/f	1,375	33

Journal

		Journal no			
		Date _____			
		Prepared by _____			
Code	Account	Debit		Credit	
———	———————	———	———	———	———
———	———————	———	———	———	———
———	———————	———	———	———	———
———	———————	———	———	———	———
———	———————	———	———	———	———
———	———————	———	———	———	———
———	———————	———	———	———	———
———	———————	———	———	———	———
———	———————	———	———	———	———
———	———————	———	———	———	———
———	———————	———	———	———	———
———	———————	———	———	———	———
———	———————	———	———	———	———
———	———————	———	———	———	———
———	———————	———	———	———	———
———	———————	———	———	———	———
———	———————	———	———	———	———
———	———————	———	———	———	———
———	———————	———	———	———	———
TOTALS		———	———	———	———
NARRATIVE					

Code	Account	Debit		Credit	
		Journal no			
		Date _____			
		Prepared by _____			
_____	_____	____	____	____	____
_____	_____	____	____	____	____
_____	_____	____	____	____	____
_____	_____	____	____	____	____
_____	_____	____	____	____	____
_____	_____	____	____	____	____
_____	_____	____	____	____	____
_____	_____	____	____	____	____
_____	_____	____	____	____	____
_____	_____	____	____	____	____
_____	_____	____	____	____	____
_____	_____	____	____	____	____
_____	_____	____	____	____	____
_____	_____	____	____	____	____
_____	_____	____	____	____	____
_____	_____	____	____	____	____
_____	_____	____	____	____	____
_____	_____	____	____	____	____
TOTALS		____	____	____	____
NARRATIVE					

DEHLAVI KOSMETATOS

388 Commercial Road Bristol BS1 3UH
Tel: 01272 755644

STATEMENT OF ACCOUNT

| Customer name | Natural Products Ltd | Customer account no 090 |
| Customer address | 151 Green Lane Taunton TA20 6GH | |

Statement date 31 January 20X1		Dr		Cr		Balance	
Date	Transaction	£	p	£	p	£	p
1/1/X1	Balance b/f	656	30			656	30
4/1/X1	Payment - thank you			645	10	11	20
24/1/X1	Invoice 2356	471	28			482	48
30/1/X1	Invoice 2389	399	40			881	88
Balance						881	88

MAIN LEDGER LISTING - EXTRACT

Supplier codes

B103	Bruning & Soler
D101	Dehlavi Kosmetatos
E103	James Ellington
G103	Greig Handling
H102	Hartley Chemicals
M102	Mortimer, Hassell
N101	Natural Ingredients
R102	Rendell & Sayers

Liabilities

020	Trade creditors
022	VAT control account

Purchases

151	Oils and waxes
152	Essential oils
153	Emulsifiers and preservatives
154	Colours

Purchases returns

161	Oils and waxes
162	Essential oils
163	Emulsifiers and preservatives
164	Colours

PRACTICE DEVOLVED ASSESSMENT 3
TOYBOX GAMES LTD

Performance criteria covered

Element 2.2 Prepare authorised payments

- ◆ Payments are correctly calculated from relevant documentation

- ◆ Payments are scheduled and authorised by the appropriate person

- ◆ Queries are referred to the appropriate person

- ◆ Security and confidentiality are maintained according to organisational requirements

Range

Payments
- ◆ petty cash

Documentation
- ◆ petty cash claims

DATA AND TASKS

The situation and the tasks to be completed are set out on the following pages.

The simulation is divided into **seven tasks**.

This booklet also contains a large amount of data which you may need to complete the tasks. You are advised to read the whole of the simulation before commencing as all of the information may be of value and is not necessarily supplied in the sequence in which you might wish to deal with it.

A high level of accuracy is required. Check your work carefully before handing it in.

Correcting fluid may be used but it should be used in moderation. Errors should be crossed out neatly and clearly You should write in black ink, not pencil.

Documents provided

Completed copies of internal and other documents	-	Petty cash schedule
	-	Petty cash vouchers
Internal ledgers	-	Petty cash book (payments)
	-	Journal
	-	Main ledger accounts
Blank copies of internal forms	-	Petty cash reconciliation
	-	Cheque requisition
	-	Memorandum
Other internal information	-	Main ledger coding (extract)

THE SITUATION

Business name	Toybox Games Ltd
Location	Bristol
Business	Manufacture and wholesale of children's and adults' board games

Business profile

The business was started in 1924 by George Wellington, grandfather of the present sales director.

The company was bought in 1985 by Perfect Leisure plc, a large toy and game company listed on the stock exchange.

The company expanded considerably in the 1980s when it successfully introduced the game *Trivialisation*.

Personnel

Managing director	Andrew Pritchard

Department heads

Production director	Ian Grahamson
Buying director	Eric Connelly
Sales director	Derek Gibb
Management accountant	Sarah Chesterton

Accounts function

Accounts assistant	Andrew Donnelly
Credit controller	Stanley Green
Cashier	You

Accounts function

The company has entirely manual systems although they will become computerised in line with the rest of the group next year.

Procedures

Here is an extract from the group's procedures manual.

Petty cash

1   The main source of petty cash is cheques drawn on the main bank account. An imprest system is maintained. (Levels of cash held are set locally.)

2   Petty cash can only be paid out on the production of a petty cash voucher authorised by a department head.

In addition there are authorisation limits for each department head of £100.00. Any amount over £100.00 must be authorised by the managing director.

All petty cash vouchers over £5.00 must be supported by receipts/invoices (even if these are not proper VAT receipts/invoices).

Petty cash will not be paid out if the above rules are not followed.

3   Correctly completed petty cash vouchers must be numbered and correctly filed. If a voucher cannot be coded it must not be numbered or written up and the cash will not be paid.

4   Expenditure must be correctly coded and analysed in the petty cash book. The analysis must be performed at the same time as the petty cash book is written up.

VAT may only be reclaimed where the company holds a proper VAT invoice/receipt.

5   The petty cash book must be written up weekly. The balance of cash in hand must be reconciled to the records.

A cheque requisition must be completed for the balance needed to restore the level of cash held.

6   A journal must be prepared to post the totals of expenditure to the correct main ledger accounts.

Terms of trade

The company is registered for VAT. All sales of board games are standard-rated.

THE TASKS TO BE COMPLETED

Today is 4 December 20X1.

TASK 1   Produce a schedule of vouchers that cannot be paid, giving reasons for non-payment.

TASK 2   Write up the petty cash book to 30 November 20X1 from the acceptable vouchers provided. The last voucher before this batch was number 334.

TASK 3   Prepare a journal entry to post totals of expenditure to the correct ledger accounts. The last journal was number 3345.

TASK 4   Using the journal entry, post totals of expenditure to the correct main ledger accounts.

TASK 5   Reconcile the balance of petty cash held to the petty cash records using the petty cash reconciliation.

TASK 6   Prepare a cheque requisition to restore the level of cash held to £100.00.

TASK 7   Any discrepancies arising in the above tasks must be documented in a memorandum to Sarah Chesterton.

PETTY CASH SCHEDULE OF CASH IN HAND AT 30 NOVEMBER 20X1

£10	notes	2
£5	notes	4
£1	coins	12
50p	coins	1
20p	coins	1
10p	coins	1
2p	coins	1

PETTY CASH VOUCHER

Authorised by DG		Received by		Code		No	
Date	Description				Amount		
25/11	flowers for D Gibbs					16	99
	Secretary						
				Total		16	99

No receipt is available.

PETTY CASH VOUCHER

Authorised by SAC		Received by		Code		No	
Date	Description				Amount		
30/11	Coffee / tea					6	51
	Finance dept						
				Total		6	51

A receipt is available but it is not a proper VAT receipt.

PETTY CASH VOUCHER				
Authorised by *DG*		Received by	Code	No
Date	Description		Amount	
30/11	Biscuits / coffee / sugar		6	78
	Sales & Marketing			
	Kitchen			
		Total	6	78

A proper VAT receipt is available. VAT of 30 pence is recoverable.

PETTY CASH VOUCHER				
Authorised by *DG*		Received by	Code	No
Date	Description		Amount	
28/11	Coffee / milk		3	51
	Production			
		Total	3	51

PETTY CASH VOUCHER

Authorised by SAC	Received by	Code		No	
Date	Description	Amount			
28/11	Stamps –			3	68
	Finance dept (franking				
	machine empty)				
	Total			3	68

PETTY CASH VOUCHER

Authorised by DG	Received by	Code		No	
Date	Description	Amount			
27/11	Sales conference			12	99
	– Taxi home to station				
	Total			12	99

A receipt is available.

PETTY CASH VOUCHER

Authorised by EJC	Received by	Code	No		
Date	Description		Amount		
28/11	Food for staff party			13	71
	- Buying Department				
		Total		13	71

A proper VAT receipt is available - VAT of £1.50 reclaimable.

PETTY CASH VOUCHER

Authorised by DG	Received by	Code	No		
Date	Description		Amount		
27/11	Sales conference			179	00
	- Rail tickets				
		Total		179	00

A receipt is available.

PETTY CASH VOUCHER

Authorised by *IG*	Received by		Code		No	
Date	Description			Amount		
30/11	*Window cleaner*				7	00
		Total			7	00

A receipt is available. The window-cleaner is not registered for VAT. There is no code for this expense.

PETTY CASH VOUCHER

Authorised by	Received by		Code		No	
Date	Description			Amount		
26/11	*VAT Book-*				15	78
	Finance Dept					
		Total			15	78

A receipt is available.

PETTY CASH BOOK

Date	Voucher number	£		£ 01 Sales	£ 02 Production	£ 03 Buying	£ 04 Finance	£ VAT	Code

JOURNAL	PETTY CASH EXPENDITURE		No	

Prepared by _____   Week ending _____

Authorised by _____

Department	Expense	Account code	Debit	Credit
Sales / marketing	Entertainment	01 06 01 20		
	Education	21		
	Travelling	22		
	Welfare	23		
	Stationery/Post	24		
Production	Entertainment	01 06 02 20		
	Education	21		
	Travelling	22		
	Welfare	23		
	Stationery/Post	24		
Buying	Entertainment	01 06 03 20		
	Education	21		
	Travelling	22		
	Welfare	23		
	Stationery/Post	24		
Finance	Entertainment	01 06 04 20		
	Education	21		
	Travelling	22		
	Welfare	23		
	Stationery/Post	24		
VAT		02 08 90 00		
Petty cash		01 05 10 00		
TOTALS				

MAIN LEDGER

Account name *Sales/marketing - Entertainment*   Account no   *0120*

31/10/X1	*b/f*	*2.385.91*

Account name *Sales/ marketing - Travel*   Account no   *0122*

17/11/X1	*b/f*	*1.395.28*
24/11/X1	*3329*	*28.30*

Account name *Sales / marketing - Welfare*   Account no   *0123*

MAIN LEDGER

Production - Welfare   0223

Account name   Account no

24/11/X1	b/f	391.18

Buying - Welfare   0323

Account name   Account no

24/11/X1	b/f	316.16

Finance - Welfare   0423

Account name   Account no

24/11/X1	b/f	399.08

MAIN LEDGER

Finance stationery / postage　　　　0424
Account name ─────────────────── Account no ──────────

| 24/11/X1 | b/f | 399.80 |

Petty cash　　　　01051000
Account name ─────────────────── Account no ──────────

1/11/X1	b/f	100.00	10/11/X1	3301	78.50
13/11/X1	3303	78.50	17/11/X1	3314	58.80
20/11/X1	3315	58.80	24/11/X1	3329	77.03
27/11/X1	3330	77.03			

VAT control account　　　　02089000
Account name ─────────────────── Account no ──────────

| | | | 24/11/X1 | b/f | 20,935.86 |

PETTY CASH RECONCILIATION

Date _____   Prepared by _____

                                Authorised by _____

                                                          £

Cash per cash book

    Balance brought forward   _____

    Receipts   _____

    Payments   _____

    Balance carried forward   _____

Cash in hand   _____

Difference   _____

CHEQUE REQUISITION

Company _____   Voucher no _____

Amount £ _____   Date _____

Payee _____

Purpose _____

_____

_____

Signed _____   Authorised _____

Payment date_____   Cheque no _____

MEMORANDUM

To:
From:
Subject:
Date:

MAIN LEDGER CODING (Extract)

Sundry administrative expenditure

	Department codes		*Expense types*
010601	Sales and marketing	20	Entertaining
010602	Production	21	Education and training
010603	Buying	22	Travel and subsistence
010604	Finance	23	Staff welfare
		24	Stationery and postage

Value added tax

020890	VAT control account	00	All departments

Petty cash

010510	Petty cash control account	00	All departments

PRACTICE DEVOLVED ASSESSMENT 4

JP HARTNELL LTD (2)

Performance criteria covered

Element 2.2 Prepare authorised payments

♦ Payments are correctly calculated from relevant documentation

♦ Payments are scheduled and authorised by the appropriate person

♦ Queries are referred to the appropriate person

♦ Security and confidentiality are maintained according to organisational requirements

Range

Payments

♦ creditors

Documentation

♦ suppliers' statements

♦ cheque requisitions

DATA AND TASKS

The situation and the tasks to be completed are set out on the following pages.

The simulation is divided into **nine** tasks.

This booklet also contains a large amount of data which you may need to complete the tasks. You are advised to read the whole of the simulation before commencing as all of the information may be of value and is not necessarily supplied in the sequence in which you might wish to deal with it.

A high level of accuracy is required. Check your work carefully before handing it in.

Correcting fluid may be used but it should be used in moderation. Errors should be crossed out neatly and clearly. You should write in black ink, not pencil.

Documents provided

Documents received from suppliers	-	Invoices
Blank copies of other documents	-	Cheques
	-	Cheques paid listing
	-	Remittance advices

THE SITUATION

Business name	JP Hartnell Ltd
Location	Four manufacturing and distribution sites in Warrington, Consett, Hastings and Solihull
	Head office in Milton Keynes
Business	Manufacture and distribution of doors

Business profile

Each of the four manufacturing and distribution sites is responsible for its own purchases of goods and services from suppliers (including heat, light and power).

Each site also pays its own wages and salaries.

Solihull site

The Solihull site manufactures the company's full range of doors and distributes them with its fleet of lorries.

Personnel

Operations manager	Neil McCann
Finance manager	Paul Snow
Accounts assistant	You

One of your responsibilities is the preparation of cheques to send to suppliers.

Procedures

1   All invoices are stamped immediately on receipt and passed to Paul Snow for **authorisation**.

2   Paul Snow authorises the invoices (shown by his signature) and **codes** them (for head office's use).

3   Invoices are returned to you to check the accuracy of the calculations (clerical accuracy).

4   For accurate invoices which have been correctly authorised and coded **only**, you write out **cheques** and prepare **remittance advices**.

5   Cheques are listed on a **cheques paid listing** and the **date paid** is written on the face of the invoices and the cheques paid listing.

6   Cheques are then passed to **both** Neil McCann and Paul Snow for signature along with the invoices and the cheques paid listing.

7   The cheques paid listing is sent to head office each Friday afternoon with the related invoices.

Terms of trade

Certain of the company's suppliers offer settlement discounts.

The company is registered for VAT.

THE TASKS TO BE COMPLETED

Today is 20 September 20X1.

You are required to prepare a batch of cheques to send to suppliers. You must follow the company's procedures as described above.

TASK 1	Check the calculations of the invoices returned to you by Paul Snow and produce a schedule of invoices indicating those which have errors or do not conform to the company's procedures.
TASK 2	Write out cheques for invoices that conform to the company's procedures.
TASK 3	Fill out the cheques paid listing. The last sequential number for these was 94.
TASK 4	Complete the remittance advices for the cheques paid to suppliers of goods.
TASK 5	What should happen to invoices which are

        (a)   not authorised?

        (b)   not coded?

        (c)   inaccurate?

TASK 6	You have drawn up a batch of cheques ready for signature, but one of the directors is on holiday. Suggest an alternative procedure for cheque signing in such circumstances.
TASK 7	Cheques prepared are sent with the **cheques paid listing** for signature. Why is the list sent as well?
	Suggest one way in which Paul Snow could check that all the cheques written are recorded on the listing.
TASK 8	In writing out one of the cheques, you have made an error. How must you deal with the cheque?
TASK 9	For any invoices that were clerically inaccurate, draft an appropriate letter to the supplier to be sent from Paul Snow.

Sale N4598

Brown and Hargraves Limited

Taxpoint 7 September 20X1

405 Railway Road
Solihull
B90 4SD

Tel: 0121 237 8966

Vat reg no 348 9876 49

Customer

JP Hartnell Limited
Thelwell Works, Thelwell Road,
Solihull B90 0AY

Description	Unit price £	Total £
Mahogany interior (premium)		
11 pieces		
2440 × 1220mm (18mm)	246.75	2,714.25
Value added tax at 17.5%		474.99
		3,189.24

CENTRAL MANAGEMENT
N/L CODE 1901
APPROVED P. Snow

ENGLISH GAS plc

English Gas plc
West Midlands
PO Box 38
Birmingham
B60 4HU

COMMERCIAL USER QUARTERLY BILLING

J P Hartnell
Thelwell Works
SOLIHULL
B90 0AY

Account reference
2345 7834 1234 HA

Enquiries
0121 236 4656

VAT REGISTRATION No 273 4455 23

Meter reading		Gas supplied		Pence			VAT
Present	Previous	Cubic feet	Therms	per Therm		£	rate
0563	0342	221	227.409	39.8		90.51	17.5%

STANDING CHARGE — 8.70 17.5%

99.21

CENTRAL MANAGEMENT
N/L CODE 907
APPROVED P. Snow

TOTAL (EXCL VAT) £99.21   **VAT** £17.36   £116.57

Date of reading	Date of account (Taxpoint)	Calorific value
29 8 X1	31 8 X1	38.4 MJ/m³ (1029 BTUs/cu ft)

- -

Customer reference number
2345 7834 1234 HA

bank giro credit

*Cashier's stamp
and initials*

Signature

Date

42 - 56 - 67
Sterling Bank plc
Head office
collection account

Cash

Cheques

Total

BILL WITH BANK GIRO CREDIT ATTACHED

ENGLISH TELECOMM plc

Customer account number
1432 5768 T6
6/9/X1
(TAXPOINT)

VAT REG No 287 5784 37

Accounts Department
PO Box 374
Birmingham
B60 3JF

J P Hartnell
Thelwell Works
SOLIHULL
B90 0AY

For enquiries dial 230 and ask for commercial accounts

CHARGES FOR TELEPHONE SERVICE ON 0121 345 3654

	£	£
CURRENT CHARGES		
Rental and other charges - see stmt	117.63	
Total of current charges (exc VAT)	117.63	
Value Added Tax at 17.50%	20. 59	
Total of Current charges (inc VAT)		138.22

CENTRAL MANAGEMENT
N/L CODE 906
APPROVED P. Snow

| Total amount due | | 138.22 |

PLEASE USE RETURN ENVELOPE FOR PAYMENT

- -

Customer account number
1432 5768 T6

bank giro credit

Cashier's stamp
and initials

Date

_____
Signature

Cash	
Cheques	
Total	

78 - 58 - 35
Financial Bank plc
Head office
collection account

H. Freeman Timber Suppliers

Sales Invoice 2837H

Freeman Yard, Porchester Way, Solihull B90 2HJ

VAT registration number 360 3395 83

Taxpoint 19 08 X1

Sale to:

> J P. Hartnell Limited
> Thelwell Works
> Thelwell Road
> SOLIHULL
> B90 0AY

100 sheets plyboard 1220 x 613 mm at £21.89	£2,189.00
VAT at 17.5%	£383.08
Total	£2,572.08

Hardy Supplies Limited

228 Thornton Lane, London W12 9ER Tel: 020 8740 6712
Depots at: Shepherd's Bush, Solihull, Salford

Invoice no 12701   **Taxpoint 3 - 9 - X1**

VAT registration number 360 3395 83

Sale to:

> J.P. Hartnell Limited
> Thelwell Works
> Thelwell Road
> SOLIHULL
> B90 0AY

200 sheets chipboard 2440 x 914mm at £16.75   £3,650.00

VAT at 17.5%   £586.25

Total   £4,236.25

CENTRAL MANAGEMENT	
N/L CODE	902
APPROVED	P. Snow

Newman and Royston Limited

Dove Works, Thelwell Road, Solihull B90 0AY

Tel: 0121 569 2984

457

CUSTOMER ADDRESS

J P. Hartnell Limited

Thelwell Works

Thelwell Road

SOLIHULL

B90 0AY

DATE: 12 SEPTEMBER 20X1

Sale

Description	Unit price	Total
10 lbs carpentry nails	£2.45	£24.50

Terms of trade

1.5% discount on invoices paid within 14 days

Please send to the above address

Original Brass Fitting Company Limited

63 Hollowtree Road, Wallsend, Newcastle, NE23 6TY
Tel   0191 345 7217 Fax: 0191 345 7296

INVOICE 74184
Taxpoint 12/9/X1
VAT Reg No 456 2283 97

To:
J.P Hartnell Limited
Thelwell Works
Thelwell Road
SOLIHULL
B90 0AY

Sale:	£
200 brass door handles (Victorian) @ £20.25 each	4,050 00
Less cash discount	81.00
	3,969 00
VAT at 17.5%	694 58
Total Payable	4,663 58

Terms of trade
2% for payment within 14 days

Remittance advice

J P Hartnell
Thelwell Works
Thelwell Road
SOLIHULL
B90 0AY

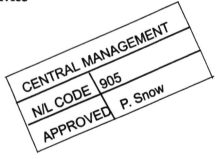

CENTRAL MANAGEMENT
N/L CODE   905
APPROVED P. Snow

INVOICE NO	DATE	AMOUNT	DISCOUNT
74184	12/9/X1	£4,744 58	

Original Brass Fitting Company Limited

63 Hollowtree Road, Wallsend, Newcastle, NE23 6TY
Tel: 0191 345 7217 Fax: 0191 345 7296

INVOICE 74378
Taxpoint 15/9/X1
VAT Reg No 456 2283 97

To:
J.P Hartnell Limited
Thelwell Works
Thelwell Road
SOLIHULL
B90 0AY

Sale	£
100 brass door handles (Victorian) @ £20 25 each	2,025 00
Less cash discount	40.50
	1,984 50
VAT at 17 5%	340.34
Total Payable	2,324.84

Terms of trade
2% for payment within 14 days

Remittance advice

J P Hartnell
Thelwell Works
Thelwell Road
SOLIHULL
B90 0AY

INVOICE NO	DATE	AMOUNT	DISCOUNT
74378	15/9/X1	£2,365 34	

Original Brass Fitting Company Limited

63 Hollowtree Road, Wallsend, Newcastle, NE23 6TY
Tel: 0191 345 7217 Fax: 0191 345 7296

INVOICE 74183
Taxpoint 12/9/X1
VAT Reg No 456 2283 97

To:
J P Hartnell Limited
Thelwell Works
Thelwell Road
SOLIHULL
B90 0AY

CENTRAL MANAGEMENT
N/L CODE 905
APPROVED P. Snow

	£
Sale:	
300 brass door handles	6,075 00
(Victorian)	
@ £20.25 each	
Less cash discount	121 50
	5,953 50
VAT at 17.5%	1,041 86
Total Payable	6,995.36

Terms of trade
2% for payment within 14 days

Remittance advice

J P Hartnell
Thelwell Works
Thelwell Road
SOLIHULL
B90 0AY

INVOICE NO	DATE	AMOUNT	DISCOUNT
74183	12/9/X1	£7,116 86	

NO 6679

Parker and Fellows Supplies

Please send your remittance to:

Centurion House
23 Railway Road
SOLIHULL
B90 4SD   Tel: 0121 567 3948

Tax point 2/9/X1

VAT REG NO 163 8876 91

Sale to:
J P Hartnell Limited
Thelwell Works
Thelwell Road
SOLIHULL

DESCRIPTION	UNIT PRICE £	TOTAL £
Veneered blockwood interior 150 sheets 2440 mm x 1220 mm (18 mm)	49 75	7,462 50
Value Added Tax at 17 5% (on discounted price)		1,279 82
		8,742 32

Invoices paid within 30 days carry a 2% discount

Remittance advice

From J P Hartnell, Thelwell Works, Thelwell Road, Solihull

Invoice 6679   £8,742 32   Discount £149 25

_____Date	
_____Payee	**STERLING BANK PLC** ## - ## - ##
_____	SOLIHULL BRANCH
_____	46 FAIRWAY SOLIHULL B90 3RD _____
_____	
_____	Pay or order
£ _____	£
000123	J P HARTNELL LTD
	000123 ## - ## - ## #########

_____Date	
_____Payee	**STERLING BANK PLC** ## - ## - ##
_____	SOLIHULL BRANCH
_____	46 FAIRWAY SOLIHULL B90 3RD _____
_____	
_____	Pay or order
£ _____	£
000124	J P HARTNELL LTD
	000124 ## - ## - ## #########

_____Date	
_____Payee	**STERLING BANK PLC** ## - ## - ##
_____	SOLIHULL BRANCH
_____	46 FAIRWAY SOLIHULL B90 3RD _____
_____	
_____	Pay or order
£ _____	£
000125	J P HARTNELL LTD
	000125 ## - ## - ## #########

Date

Payee

£

000126

STERLING BANK PLC

SOLIHULL BRANCH
46 FAIRWAY SOLIHULL B90 3RD

- ## -

Pay

or order

£

J P HARTNELL LTD

000126   ## - ## - ##   #########

Date

Payee

£

000127

STERLING BANK PLC

SOLIHULL BRANCH
46 FAIRWAY SOLIHULL B90 3RD

- ## -

Pay

or order

£

J P HARTNELL LTD

000127   ## - ## - ##   #########

Date

Payee

£

000128

STERLING BANK PLC

SOLIHULL BRANCH
46 FAIRWAY SOLIHULL B90 3RD

- ## -

Pay

or order

£

J P HARTNELL LTD

000128   ## - ## - ##   #########

_____ Date

_____ Payee

_____

_____

_____

£ _____

000129

STERLING BANK PLC

SOLIHULL BRANCH
46 FAIRWAY SOLIHULL B90 3RD

- ## -

_____

Pay _____ or order

£

J P HARTNELL LTD

000129   ## - ## - ##   #########

_____ Date

_____ Payee

_____

_____

_____

£ _____

000130

STERLING BANK PLC

SOLIHULL BRANCH
46 FAIRWAY SOLIHULL B90 3RD

- ## -

_____

Pay _____ or order

£

J P HARTNELL LTD

000130   ## - ## - ##   #########

_____ Date

_____ Payee

_____

_____

_____

£ _____

000131

STERLING BANK PLC

SOLIHULL BRANCH
46 FAIRWAY SOLIHULL B90 3RD

- ## -

_____

Pay _____ or order

£

J P HARTNELL LTD

000131   ## - ## - ##   #########

Cheques Paid Listing

Date _____

Site _____

No_____

Prepared by _____

Supplier	Invoice No	Cheque No	Amount £		Discount taken £	
		Total				

REMITTANCE ADVICE		
From: J P Hartnell Limited Thelwell Works Thelwell Road Solihull B90 0AY **Tel: 0121 667 3993**		
To:		
Date:		
Details of invoices, etc	Amount	
Cheque no enclosed		

REMITTANCE ADVICE		
From: J P Hartnell Limited Thelwell Works Thelwell Road Solihull B90 0AY **Tel: 0121 667 3993**		
To:		
Date:		
Details of invoices, etc	Amount	
Cheque no enclosed		

REMITTANCE ADVICE		
From: J P Hartnell Limited Thelwell Works Thelwell Road Solihull B90 0AY **Tel: 0121 667 3993**		
To:		
Date:		
Details of invoices, etc	Amount	
Cheque no enclosed		

REMITTANCE ADVICE		
From: **J P Hartnell Limited** **Thelwell Works** **Thelwell Road** **Solihull B90 0AY**	**Tel: 0121 667 3993**	
To:		
Date:		
Details of invoices, etc	Amount	
Cheque no enclosed		

REMITTANCE ADVICE		
From: **J P Hartnell Limited** **Thelwell Works** **Thelwell Road** **Solihull B90 0AY**	**Tel: 0121 667 3993**	
To:		
Date:		
Details of invoices, etc	Amount	
Cheque no enclosed		

REMITTANCE ADVICE		
From: **J P Hartnell Limited** **Thelwell Works** **Thelwell Road** **Solihull B90 0AY**	**Tel: 0121 667 3993**	
To:		
Date:		
Details of invoices, etc	Amount	
Cheque no enclosed		

PRACTICE DEVOLVED ASSESSMENT 5
PARK FOODS GROUP PLC

Performance criteria covered

Element 2.3 Make and record payments

♦ The appropriate payment method is used in accordance with organisational procedures

♦ Payments are made in accordance with organisational processes and timescales

♦ Payments are entered into accounting records according to organisational procedures

♦ Security and confidentiality are maintained according to organisational requirements

♦ Queries are referred to the appropriate person.

Range

Payment methods

♦ cash

♦ cheques

♦ automated payments

Payments

♦ creditors

Accounting records

♦ cash book

DATA AND TASKS

The situation and the tasks to be completed are set out on the following pages.

There are **five tasks.**

This booklet also contains a large amount of data which you may need to complete the tasks. You are advised to read the whole of the simulation before commencing as all of the information may be of value and is not necessarily supplied in the sequence in which you might wish to deal with it.

A high level of accuracy is required. Check your work carefully before handing it in.

Correcting fluid may be used but it should be used in moderation. Errors should be crossed out neatly and clearly. You should write in black ink, not pencil.

Documents provided

Completed copies of internal documents	-	Cheques paid listing
	-	Standing order schedule
	-	Direct debit schedule
	-	BACS listing
	-	Wages book summary
Internal ledgers	-	Cash book
	-	Main ledger
	-	Subsidiary ledger – purchases
	-	Journal

Blank forms

THE SITUATION

Business name	Park Foods Group plc	
Location	Head office	Coventry
	Sites	Milton Keynes
		Southampton
		Bristol
Business	Manufacture of bread, sandwiches, cakes and other confectionery	

Business profile

The original company (Park Foods Ltd) started in 1930 making cakes and biscuits. The company expanded considerably during the 1970s through the acquisition of a number of specialist confectionery companies. During the 1980s it started manufacturing sandwiches for major food retailers. The group was floated on the stock exchange in 1986.

The accounts function records all of the sales, purchases, salaries and cash transactions. Records are currently kept on a manual system.

Personnel

Financial director	Hugh Southgate
Accountant	Patricia Konig
Ledger Assistant	Sarah Oliver
Cashier	You

Monies paid

All suppliers are paid by cheque, standing order or direct debit.

Cheques are prepared and sent to the payee by the central accounts function which sends a listing of cheques paid to the site accounts function.

Salaries are normally paid by BACS, although adjustments may be made by cheque.

THE TASKS TO BE COMPLETED

Today is 4 May 20X1.

TASK 1   Write up the analysed cash book for the week ended 30 April 20X1, from the:

Cheques paid listing
Standing order schedule
Direct debit schedule
BACS listing

TASK 2   Complete the journal entry for the posting of the totals of the cash payments book.

TASK 3   Post the totals of the cash payments book to the main ledger accounts.

TASK 4   Post the individual payments to the four subsidiary ledger, (purchases) accounts given.

TASK 5   Using the wages book totals given, write up the main ledger accounts for wages for the month – the salaries expense account (the net salary paid should already have been entered), the gross salaries control account and the Inland Revenue account.

CHEQUES PAID LISTING
Milton Keynes
Cheque run 24/4/X1

Creditors

2374	Fowler & Kenworthy Ltd	17,678.67
75	Vinegar Supply Company Ltd	1,657.99
76	Western Farmers Ltd	34,766.45
77	Fish Supply Group plc	14,365.00
78	General Grain Supply Co Ltd	2,334.45
79	Tamar Flour Millers Ltd	1,766.38
80	Angus Meat Suppliers plc	5,443.12
81	Hobbs and Davies Ltd	773.56
82	Jersey Foods Ltd	3,716.33
83	Flour Products Ltd	12,674.99
84	DI Ltd	543.92
85	Finer Products Ltd	23,894.34
86	Greengates Ltd	9,333.25
87	Catering Supplies Ltd	112.32
88	Plastic Products Ltd	6,833.28
89	Simpson Foods Ltd	346.60
90	Paper Bag Company Ltd	10,004.43
91	United Food Producers Ltd	9,567.76
92	TY Foods Ltd	17,334.78
93	Bell Distribution International Ltd	3,885.38
94	Winter & White Ltd	267.56
95	Dairy Produce Company Ltd	245.87
96	Ghanwani Foods Ltd	844.20
97	Cross & Fordingham Ltd	18,794.95
98	T & P Importers Ltd	10,339.27
2399	Golden Grains Ltd	5,680.11
2400	Imperial Foods plc	605.02

Salaries

2401	L Freeborough	76.83

STANDING ORDER SCHEDULE

DATE	PAYEE	AMOUNT £	SPECIAL INSTRUCTIONS
19th Monthly	Feed producers Assoc	60.00	Last payment 19/4/X9
28th Quarterly	Kennedy Property	6,547.45	Rent of warehouse April, July, Oct & January
15th Quarterly	Northern Gas	60.65	March, June, Sept, Dec

DIRECT DEBIT SCHEDULE

DATE	PAYEE	AMOUNT £	SPECIAL INSTRUCTIONS
24th	Security Insurance	546.90	April, July, Oct, Dec
Quarterly			
27th	English Telecomm	Variable	April, July, Oct, Dec
Quarterly			

The April bill from English Telecomm totalled £378.65 inclusive of £56.39 VAT.

BACS Listing

Milton Keynes

25/4/X1

		£
Salaries	**01**	**23,564.22**
	02	**12,453.64**
	03	**35,555.25**
	04	**3,630.66**

		Cash Book Payments					
Date	Narrative	Cheque no	Total	Creditors	Salaries	Other	VAT

JOURNAL

	Journal no	78
	Date	
	Authorised	Patricia Konig
	Dr	**Cr**
Reason		

MAIN LEDGER ACCOUNTS

Creditors control account

	£			£
		23/4/X1	Balance b/f	346,589.45

Salaries expense account

		£		£
23/4/X1	Balance b/f	250,437.36		

Rent account

		£		£
23/4/X1	Balance b/f	7,235.46		

Insurance account

		£		£
23/4/X1	Balance b/f	478.69		

Telephone account

		£		£
23/4/X1	Balance b/f	412.56		

VAT account

	£			£
		23/4/X1	Balance b/f	20,376.43

Gross salaries control account

	£		£

Inland Revenue account

	£			£
		12/4/X1	Balance b/f	18,584.34

SUBSIDIARY LEDGER – PURCHASES LEDGER ACCOUNTS

Fowler & Kenworthy Ltd   2374

	£			£
		23/4/X1	Balance b/f	23,475.68

Hobbs and Davies Ltd   2381

	£			£
		23/4/X1	Balance b/f	1,043.50

Paper Bag Company Ltd   2390

	£			£
		23/4/X1	Balance b/f	10,004.43

T & P Importers Ltd   2398

	£			£
		23/4/X1	Balance b/f	15,364.89

WAGES BOOK SUMMARY

Department	Gross pay	PAYE	Employee's NIC	Employer's NIC	Net pay
	£	£	£	£	£
01	29,222.55	3,682.04	1,899.46	2,454.70	23,641.05
02	15,393.87	1,939 63	1,000.60	1,293.08	12,453.64
03	43,949.63	5,537.65	2,856.73	3,691.77	35,555.25
04	4,487.84	565.47	291.71	376.98	3,630.66
	93,053.89	11,724.79	6,048.50	7,816.53	75,280.60

PRACTICE DEVOLVED ASSESSMENT 6
NATURAL PRODUCTS LTD (2)

Performance criteria covered

Element 2.3 Make and record payments

♦ The appropriate payment method is used in accordance with organisational procedures

♦ Payments are made in accordance with organisational processes and timescales

♦ Payments are entered into accounting records according to organisational procedures

DATA AND TASKS

The situation and the tasks to be completed are set out on the following pages.

The simulation is divided into **nine** tasks.

This booklet also contains a large amount of data which you may need to complete the tasks. You are advised to read the whole of the simulation before commencing as all of the information may be of value and is not necessarily supplied in the sequence in which you might wish to deal with it.

A high level of accuracy is required. Check your work carefully before handing it in.

Correcting fluid may be used but it should be used in moderation. Errors should be crossed out neatly and clearly. You should write in black ink, not pencil.

Documents provided

Blank copies of external documents	-	Cheques
Completed copies of internal documents	-	Direct debit schedule
	-	Cheque requisitions
	-	Petty cash vouchers
Internal ledgers	-	Cash book (payments)
	-	Petty cash book (payments)
Other internal information	-	Main ledger listing (extract)

THE SITUATION

Business name	Natural Products Ltd	
Location	Taunton, Somerset	
Personnel	Managing director	Cindy Taylor
	Sales director	Jason Taylor
	Production director	Tracy Yard
	Financial director	Steve Roberts
	Secretary to directors	Carol Evans

Business   Manufacture, wholesale and mail order sale of toiletries and cosmetics

Accounts department

Accounts supervisor   Caroline Everley

Ledger Clerk   Trudi Roberts

Administration and payroll   Robert Foster

Cashier and petty cashier   You

Terms of trade

Certain suppliers offer settlement discounts.

Payments

Payee   *Methods of payment*

Most suppliers   Cheques

Electricity, gas, telephone   Direct debit

Sundry expenses   Petty cash

All cheques are written manually from cheque requisitions. All requisitions must be signed by Steve Roberts (FD).

Petty cash

All petty cash vouchers in excess of £5.00 must be accompanied by receipts. All petty cash expenditure must be authorised by Steve Roberts (FD).

THE TASKS TO BE COMPLETED

PART 1

Today is 30 June 20X1.

TASK 1   Review each cheque requisition form, ensuring it has been properly authorised.

           Prepare a cheque for each acceptable requisition using the blanks provided.

           Write the cheque number and payment date on the requisition form.

TASK 2   Write up the cash book (payments) from:

           ♦   cheques written

           ♦   direct debit schedule (June payments)

           using the cash book (payments) sheet provided.

TASK 3   Review each petty cash voucher for authorisation and decide which payments can be made. Number vouchers for which payment is made. The last voucher was number 550.

TASK 4   Write up the petty cash book (payments) for each payment using the petty cash book sheet provided.

(You are starting a new petty cash book, so you will have to set up your own columns.)

PART 2

Today is 6 July 20X1.

TASK 5   Reconcile the balance of petty cash in hand with the records as at 30 June 20X1.

Cash in hand is as follows:

£10	notes	10
£5	notes	2
£1	coins	3
50p	coins	3
20p	coins	3
5p	coins	1
2p	coins	3

TASK 6   Prepare a cheque requisition form to restore the level of petty cash held to the imprest level (£200).

You are provided with blank copies of forms for

♦ Petty cash reconciliation

♦ Cheque requisitions

for Tasks 5 and 6.

PART 3

Today is 10 July 20X1. You are going to post entries to the main ledger accounts as at 30/6/X1.

TASK 7   Prepare a journal entry to post the cash book totals to the correct main ledger accounts. The last journal was number 6110.

TASK 8   Prepare a journal entry to post the petty cash expenditure totals to the correct main ledger accounts.

TASK 9   Post the totals from journals to the correct main ledger accounts.

You are provided with blank copies of journal forms and main ledger (extracts) for tasks 7, 8 and 9.

CHEQUE REQUISITION

Date _____ 29/6/X1 _____ Voucher no _____ 340 _____

Amount £ _____ 235.55 _____ Discount £ _____

Payee _____ Arthur Chong Ltd. _____

For trade creditors, account no _____ C102 _____

Purpose _____ 7C _____

_____

_____

Signed _____ Trudi Roberts _____ Authorised _____ SAR _____

Payment date _____ Cheque no _____

CHEQUE REQUISITION

Date _____ 29/6/X1 _____ Voucher no _____ 341 _____

Amount £ _____ 469.55 _____ Discount £ _____ 23.48 _____

Payee _____ Dwyer & Co (Import) Ltd _____

For trade creditors, account no _____ D102 _____

Purpose _____ 7C _____

_____

_____

Signed _____ Trudi Roberts _____ Authorised _____ SAR _____

Payment date _____ Cheque no _____

CHEQUE REQUISITION

Date _____29/6/X1_____   Voucher no   ___342___

Amount   £___449.28___   Discount £   ___4.49___

Payee   _Eastworld Ltd_____

For trade creditors, account no   _E101_____

Purpose   _7C_____

_____

_____

Signed   _Trudi Roberts_____   Authorised   ___SAR___

Payment date _____   Cheque no   _____

SOUTHERN BANK PLC
755 HIGH STREET TAUNTON TA1 4JL

22 - 56 - 01

_____ **20X1**

Pay   or order

FOR AND ON BEHALF OF
NATURAL PRODUCTS LTD

000401   22- 56 - 01   00010990

SOUTHERN BANK PLC
755 HIGH STREET TAUNTON TA1 4JL

22 - 56 - 01

_____ **20X1**

Pay   or order

FOR AND ON BEHALF OF
NATURAL PRODUCTS LTD

000402   22- 56 - 01   00010990

SOUTHERN BANK PLC
755 HIGH STREET TAUNTON TA1 4JL

22 - 56 - 01

_____ **20X1**

Pay   or order

FOR AND ON BEHALF OF
NATURAL PRODUCTS LTD

000403   22- 56 - 01   00010990

DIRECT DEBIT SCHEDULE

FREQUENCY	PAYEE	AMOUNT £	SPECIAL INSTRUCTIONS
Monthly	English	*159.78	Paid 28th of each month
	Electricity		
	plc		
Quarterly	English	329.25	Jan/April/July/Oct
	Gas	*299.80	Revised 3 April 20X1
	plc		
Monthly	English	201.39	Revised 5 Feb 20X1
	Telecomm	*224.47	Paid 26th of each month

*These amounts are inclusive of VAT at 17½%.

DOCUMENTS

Cash Book Payments								
Date	Narrative	Cheque no	Total	Creditors	Salaries	Other	VAT control	Discount received
26/6	Blackwood Foodstuffs	389	325.99	325.99				
	Bruning & Soler	390	683 85	683.85				
	Dehlavi Kosmetatos	391	2,112.16	2,112.16				
	Environmentally Friendly	392	705 77	705.77				
	Greig Handling (import)	393	1,253.98	1,253.98				
	Halpern Freedman	394	338.11	338.11				
	Kobo Design Studio	395	500.00	500.00				
	Rayner Food Co	396	375.22	375.22				
	Year 2000 Produce Co	397	1,100.68	1,100.68				
27/6	HM Customs & Excise	398	23,599.28				23,599.28	
26/6	Petty cash	399	175.10			175.10 (P. Cash)		
28/6	Salaries - Bank Giro	400	48,995.63		48,995.63			

PETTY CASH VOUCHER			
Authorised by *SAR*	Received by	Code	No
Date	Description		Amount
29/6/X1	*Windows cleaned*		*8 - 90*
		Total	*8 - 90*

A receipt is available. The window cleaner is not registered for VAT.

PETTY CASH VOUCHER			
Authorised by *SAR*	Received by	Code	No
Date	Description		Amount
30/6/X1	*Milk and biscuits*		*3 - 99*
		Total	*3 - 99*

No receipt is available.

PETTY CASH VOUCHER

Authorised by SAR	Received by	Code	No

Date	Description		Amount
28/6/X1	Headlight bulb for		1 - 99
	works van		
		Total	1 - 99

No receipt is available.

PETTY CASH VOUCHER

Authorised by SAR	Received by	Code	No

Date	Description		Amount
28/6/X1	Travel to station		6 - 95
	- Jason Taylor		
	- Sales conference		
		Total	6 - 95

A receipt is available from the taxi company.

PETTY CASH VOUCHER			
Authorised by SAR	Received by	Code	No
Date	Description		Amount
26/6/X1	Food for staff party		8 - 29
		Total	8 - 29

A proper VAT receipt is available, showing VAT of 89 pence.

PETTY CASH VOUCHER			
Authorised by SAR	Received by	Code	No
Date	Description		Amount
29/6/X1	New cashbook (blank)		12 - 98
		Total	12 - 98

A receipt is available but it is not a proper VAT receipt.

PETTY CASH VOUCHER

Authorised by SAR	Received by	Code	No

Date	Description	Amount
29/6/X1	Staff Welfare	5 - 99
	Total	5 - 99

A proper VAT receipt is available showing VAT of 50 pence.

PETTY CASH VOUCHER

Authorised by SAR	Received by	Code	No

Date	Description	Amount
30/6/X1	Taxi fare	2 - 80
	- Peter Fraser	
	Total	2 - 80

No receipt is available.

PETTY CASH VOUCHER				
Authorised by *SAR*		Received by	Code	No
Date	Description			Amount
27/6/X1	*Paint for Painting Store*			*10 - 45*
	Paint brush set			*22 - 45*
			Total	*32 - 90*

A proper VAT receipt is available showing VAT of £4.90.

MAIN LEDGER LISTING (Extract)

Income

1	Wholesale sales
3	Mail order sales
143	Other income – rent
144	Discounts received

Expenditure

201	Wages and salaries
202	Rent and rates
208	Heat and light
209	Telephones
210	General insurance
211	Repairs and renewals
212	Building maintenance
220	Postage
221	Stationery
222	Travel and subsistence
230	Motor expenses
400	General expenses
401	Staff welfare
402	Cleaning materials
445	Bank interest
447	Loan interest
448	Discounts allowed

Assets

001	Fixed assets – property
002	Fixed assets – plant and machinery
003	Fixed assets – fixtures and fittings
010	Stock
011	Trade debtors
012	Cash at bank (current account)
013	Cash at bank (deposit account)
014	Cash in hand (petty cash)

Liabilities

020	Trade creditors
021	Hire purchase
022	VAT control account

Capital and reserves

030	Share capital
031	Share premium
032	Profit and loss account reserve

Petty Cash (payments)												
		£	£	£	£	£	£	£	£	£	£	£

PETTY CASH RECONCILIATION

Date ——————————   Prepared by ——————————

Authorised by ——————————

	£
Cash per petty cash book	
Balance brought forward	————————
Receipts	————————
Payments	————————
Balance carried forward	————————
	————————
Cash in hand	————————
Difference	————————

CHEQUE REQUISITION

Date _____ Voucher no _____

Amount £ _____ Discount £ _____

Payee _____

For trade creditors, account no _____

Purpose _____

_____

_____

Signed _____ Authorised _____

Payment date _____ Cheque no _____

CHEQUE REQUISITION

Date _____ Voucher no _____

Amount £ _____ Discount £ _____

Payee _____

For trade creditors, account no _____

Purpose _____

_____

_____

Signed _____ Authorised _____

Payment date _____ Cheque no _____

		Journal no	_____
		Date	_____
		Prepared by	_____

Code	Account	Debit		Credit	
Total					

Narrative

		Journal no	
		Date	
		Prepared by	

Code	Account	Debit		Credit	
Total					

Narrative

MAIN LEDGER

Account Name: *Discounts received*		Account No: 144	
Narrative	£	*Narrative*	£
		23/6/X1 b/f	25,651.48

Account Name: *Wages and Salaries*		Account No: 201	
Narrative	£	*Narrative*	£
31/5/X1 b/f	325,119.90		

Account Name: *Heat and Light*		Account No: 208	
Narrative	£	*Narrative*	£
23/6/X1 b/f	12,995.65		

Account Name: *Telephones*		Account No: 209	
Narrative	£	*Narrative*	£
23/6/X1 b/f	3,225.91		

| Account Name: *Repairs and Renewals* | | Account No: 211 | |
Narrative	£	Narrative	£
31/5/X1 b/f	2,001.68		

| Account Name: *Building Maintenance* | | Account No: 212 | |
Narrative	£	Narrative	£
28/2/X1 b/f	1,500.74		

| Account Name: *Stationery* | | Account No: 221 | |
Narrative	£	Narrative	£
23/6/X1 b/f	8,020.97		

| Account Name: *Travel and Subsistence* | | Account No: 222 | |
Narrative	£	Narrative	£
23/6/X1 b/f	10,255.65		

Account Name: *Motor Expenses*		Account No: 230	
Narrative	£	Narrative	£
16/6/X1 b/f	5,885.94		

Account Name: *Staff Welfare*		Account No: 401	
Narrative	£	Narrative	£
23/6/X1 b/f	4,110.28		

Account Name: *Cash at bank (current)*		Account No: 012	
Narrative	£	Narrative	£
23/6/X1 b/f	84,579.77		

Account Name: *Cash in Hand*		Account No: 014	
Narrative	£	Narrative	£
23/6/X1 b/f	24.90		

Account Name: *Trade Creditors*		**Account No:** 020	
Narrative	£	*Narrative*	£
		23/6/X1 b/f	367,251.44

Account Name: *VAT Control Account*		**Account No:** 022	
Narrative	£	*Narrative*	£
		23/6/X1 b/f	22,987.38

AAT UNIT 2

MOCK DEVOLVED ASSESSMENT 1

HIS 'n' HERS FASHIONS

QUESTIONS

DATA AND TASKS

Instructions

This simulation is designed to test your ability to make and record payments.

You are allowed **three hours** to complete your work.

The situation is provided on the next page.

The simulation is divided into three parts, each containing tasks. You are advised to look through the whole simulation first to gain a general appreciation of your tasks.

Part one: Purchase Invoices

Task 1   Checking supplier invoices

Task 2   Dealing with queries

Task 3   Entering up the Day Book

Part two: Payments

Task 4   Calculation of discount

Task 5   Writing out cheques

Task 6   Writing up Cash Book

Part three: Writing up the ledgers

Task 7   Posting to Subsidiary (Purchases) Ledger

Task 8   Posting to Main Ledger

Task 9   Supplier statement reconciliation

Your answers should be set out in the answer booklet using the specimen forms provided.

A high level of accuracy is required. Check your work carefully before handing it in.

THE SITUATION

You are employed as an accounts clerk for His 'n' Hers Fashions, a wholesaler of ladies' and men's clothing. The company address is:

His 'n' Hers Fashions
27-29 Riverside
St Philips
BRISTOL
BS1 8SN

Telephone 0117 9230460
Fax 0117 9230462

The department in which you work maintains both the sales and purchases ledgers. The accounts supervisor is Carole Evans.

Your main roles are:

♦ To check invoices received from suppliers. This involves checking the invoice details against goods received notes and against the purchase orders. You are provided with a list of suppliers and the trade discount that they each offer. Goods received notes should have been authorised by the Stores Manager, Keith Winslow, and the purchase orders should have been signed by the Chief Buyer, Sarah McMahon. You should also check the invoices for numerical accuracy.

♦ Maintaining the sales, sales returns, purchases and purchase returns day books as well as the main ledger accounts. Invoices are entered up in weekly batches. Any documents without the necessary authorisation must be referred back to the appropriate personnel and must **not** be processed.

The main ledger accounts used include the following:

♦ Purchases – ladieswear (Note: items of ladieswear have a code beginning LW)

♦ Purchases – menswear (Note: items of menswear have a code beginning MW)

♦ Purchase ledger control

♦ VAT

♦ Discounts received

The company does not maintain separate sales returns and purchase returns accounts, but posts these through the sales and purchase accounts. Subsidiary (sales and purchases) ledgers are maintained for memorandum purposes only.

The date is Friday 29 March 20X1 and you are to complete all the processing of documents for the week.

THE TASKS TO BE COMPLETED

PART ONE

TASK 1

You are required to check each of the invoices given to the purchase orders and goods received notes and decide on their validity for authorisation. Any invoices that you do not consider should be authorised should be reported to the Accounts Supervisor, Carole Evans, on the memorandum provided in the answer booklet.

TASK 2

For one of the invoices that you were unable to authorise for payment in task 1 write a letter to the supplier concerned explaining the problem on the blank letterhead provided in the answer booklet.

TASK 3

Write up the purchases day book given in the answer booklet for the invoices that you did pass for payment. Total all of the columns.

PART TWO

TASK 4

Refer to the payments schedule given and calculate the amount of the payment that should be made to these two suppliers given that the payments are being made in the timescale required in order to qualify for the settlement discounts offered. Prepare your calculations on the Payments Working Schedule given in the answer booklet.

TASK 5

On the blank cheques given in the answer booklet write out the cheques and cheque counterfoil for these two payments ensuring that all information required to write up the Cash Payments Book is included on the cheque counterfoil.

TASK 6

Enter the two payments made to these two suppliers in the Cash Payments Book, given in the answer booklet. Total all of the columns.

PART THREE

TASK 7

Post all the correctly authorised invoices and the two payments above to the appropriate subsidiary (purchases) ledger accounts given in the answer booklet.

TASK 8

Post all the day book totals to the appropriate main ledger accounts given in the answer booklet.

TASK 9

You have received a statement from Look C Fashions, given. You are required to reconcile the account for Look C Fashions with the supplier statement (see the answer booklet). Draft a memo to the accounts supervisor to explain any differences that you find using the memorandum header in the answer booklet.

EXTRACT FROM LIST OF SUPPLIERS

Name	Address	Trade Discount
Look C Fashions	36 Fore Street Trowbridge Wiltshire BA14 8QF	5%
Rainbow Wholesalers	15 Union Street Bristol BS1 5BW	12.5%
Saver and Spender	12 Rodney Walk Cheltenham Gloucester GL50 6DX	5%
H I P Spinner	The Triangle Clevedon North East Somerset BS21 7NT	7.5%
I M Wilcox	4 New Road Chippenham Wiltshire SN15 4DW	12.5%

PART ONE, TASK 1

INVOICE

Rainbow Wholesalers
15 Union Street
BRISTOL BS1 5BW

VAT Reg No   910 1324 17

Invoice to

His 'n' Hers Fashions 27-29 Riverside St Philips BRISTOL BS1 8SN

Invoice no: 841

Account: P974

Date/tax point: 27 Mar 20X1

Your ref: 745

Deliver to

12½%

Code	Description	Unit size	Quantity	Price £ p	Total £ p	Discount £ p	Net amount £ p
MW 34 43	Bleached jeans, blue	30	8	17.00	136.00	17.00	119.00
MW 34 43	" " "	32	10	17.00	170.00	21.25	148.75
MW 34 43	" " "	34	12	17.00	204.00	25.50	178.50

TERMS

NET MONTHLY

CARRIAGE PAID

E & OE

TOTAL GOODS	446.25
CASH DISCOUNT	-
SUBTOTAL	446.25
VAT (17½%)	118.09
AMOUNT DUE	564.34

PART ONE, TASK 1, CONTINUED

INVOICE

Saver and Spender
12 Rodney Walk
Cheltenham
GLOS GL50 6DX

VAT Reg No   907 6420 512

Invoice to

His 'n' Hers Fashions 27-29 Riverside St Philips BRISTOL BS1 8SN

Invoice no: 5109

Account: HF87

Date/tax point: 27 Mar 20X1

Your ref: 734

Deliver to

5%

Code	Description	Unit size	Quantity	Price £ p	Total £ p	Discount £ p	Net amount £ p
MW 70 60	Sweatshirt, blue	S	10	8.50	85.00	4.25	80.75
MW 70 60	" "	M	12	8.50	102 00	5.10	96.90
MW 70 60	" "	L	8	8.50	68.00	3.40	64.60
MW 15 52	Collarless shirt, white	S	12	8.75	105.00	5.25	99.75
MW 15 52	" " "	M	14	8.75	122.50	6.13	116.37
MW 15 52	" " "	L	8	8.75	70.00	3.50	66.50

TERMS

NET MONTHLY

CARRIAGE PAID

E & OE

TOTAL GOODS	524.87
CASH DISCOUNT	-
SUBTOTAL	524.87
VAT (17½%)	91.85
AMOUNT DUE	616.72

PART ONE, TASK 1, CONTINUED

INVOICE

Look C Fashions
36 Fore Street
Trowbridge
Wilts BA14 8QF

VAT Reg No   617 2394 408

Invoice to

| His 'n' Hers Fashions |
| 27-29 Riverside |
| St Philips |
| BRISTOL BS1 8SN |

Invoice no: 01428

Account: 098

Date/tax point: 27 Mar 20X1

Your ref: 748

Deliver to

5%

Code	Description	Unit size	Quantity	Price £ p	Total £ p	Discount £ p	Net amount £ p
LW 56 01	Jogging suit, black	10/12	12	9.00	108.00	5.40	102.60
LW 56 01	" " "	14/16	15	9.00	135.00	6.75	128.25
LW 56 00	Jogging suit, purple	10/12	8	9.00	72.00	3.60	68.40
LW 56 00	" " "	14/16	10	9.00	90.00	4.50	85.50

TERMS

NET MONTHLY

CARRIAGE PAID

E & OE

TOTAL GOODS	384.75
CASH DISCOUNT	-
SUBTOTAL	384.75
VAT (17½%)	67.33
AMOUNT DUE	452.08

PART ONE, TASK 1, CONTINUED

INVOICE

H I P Spinner
The Triangle, Clevedon
North East Somerset BS21 7NT

VAT Reg No   103 1781 658

Invoice to

His 'n' Hers Fashions 27-29 Riverside St Philips BRISTOL BS1 8SN

Invoice no: 1039

Account: 7132

Date/tax point: 27 Mar 20X1

Your ref: 724

Deliver to

7½%

Code	Description	Unit size	Quantity	Price £ p	Total £ p	Discount £ p	Net amount £ p
MW 54 50	Hopsack trousers, brown	34	5	12.50	62.50	4.69	57.81
MW 57 76	" " blue	36	4	12.50	50.00	3.75	46.25
MW 43 05	Pleated cord trousers, grey	32	8	14.00	112.00	8.40	103.60
MW 47 76	Pleated baggy trousers, black	36	10	16.50	165.00	12.38	152.62

TERMS

NET MONTHLY

CARRIAGE PAID

E & OE

TOTAL GOODS	360.28
CASH DISCOUNT	-
SUBTOTAL	360.28
VAT (17½%)	63.04
AMOUNT DUE	423 32

PART ONE, TASK 1, CONTINUED

INVOICE

Rainbow Wholesalers
15 Union Street
BRISTOL BS1 5BW

VAT Reg No   910 1324 17

Invoice to

Invoice no: 838

His 'n' Hers Fashions
27-29 Riverside
St Philips
BRISTOL BS1 8SN

Account: P974

Date/tax point: 27 Mar 20X1

Your ref: 732

Deliver to

12½%

Code	Description	Unit size	Quantity	Price £ p	Total £ p	Discount £ p	Net amount £ p
LW 35 69	Stonewash jeans	10	8	15.00	120.00	15.00	105.00
LW 35 69	" "	12	12	15.00	180.00	22.50	157.50
LW 35 69	" "	14	7	15.00	105.00	13.13	91.87
LW 35 69	" "	16	3	15.00	45.00	5.63	39.37
LW 36 27	Stretch cord jeans, grey	10	6	12.00	72.00	9.00	63.00
LW 36 27	" " " "	12	8	12.00	96.00	12.00	84.00
LW 36 27	" " " "	14	4	12.00	48.00	6.00	42.00

TERMS

NET MONTHLY

CARRIAGE PAID

E & OE

TOTAL GOODS	582.74
CASH DISCOUNT	-
SUBTOTAL	582.74
VAT (17½%)	101.97
AMOUNT DUE	684.71

PART ONE, TASK 1, CONTINUED

INVOICE

I M Wilcox
4 New Road, Chippenham
WILTS SN15 4DW

VAT Reg No	298 1075 192

Invoice to

His 'n' Hers Fashions
27-29 Riverside
St Philips
BRISTOL BS1 8SN

Invoice no:	14091
Account:	929
Date/tax point:	27 Mar 20X1
Your ref:	728

Deliver to

12½%

Code	Description	Unit size	Quantity	Price £ p	Total £ p	Discount £ p	Net amount £ p
LW 50 19	Mouflon jacket, jade	12	4	32.00	128.00	16.00	112.00
LW 46 89	Wool duffle coat, purple	10	8	40.00	320.00	40.00	280.00
LW 46 87	" " " green	14	3	40.00	120.00	15.00	105.00
LW 40 80	Tweed wrapover coat, grey	16	5	32.00	160.00	20.00	140.00

TERMS

NET MONTHLY

CARRIAGE PAID

E & OE

TOTAL GOODS	637.00
CASH DISCOUNT	-
SUBTOTAL	637.00
VAT (17½%)	111.47
AMOUNT DUE	748.47

PART ONE, TASK 1, CONTINUED

INVOICE

Look C Fashions
36 Fore Street
Trowbridge
WILTS BA14 8QF

VAT Reg No   617 2394 408

Invoice to

Invoice no: 01421

His 'n' Hers Fashions
27-29 Riverside
St Philips
BRISTOL BS1 8SN

Account: 098

Date/tax point: 27 Mar 20X1

Your ref: 730

Deliver to

5%

Code	Description	Unit size	Quantity	Price £ p	Total £ p	Discount £ p	Net amount £ p
LW 55 97	Jogging suit, blue	10/12	5	9.00	45.00	2.25	42.75
LW 55 97	" " "	14/16	5	9.00	45.00	2.25	42.75
LW 55 99	" " red	10/12	10	9.00	90.00	4.50	85.50
LW 55 99	" " "	14/16	20	9.00	180.00	9.00	171.00
LW 36 16	Ski pants, black	12	15	12.00	180.00	9.00	171.00
LW 36 16	" " "	14	15	12.00	180.00	9.00	171.00

TERMS

NET MONTHLY

CARRIAGE PAID

E & OE

TOTAL GOODS	684.00
CASH DISCOUNT	-
SUBTOTAL	684.00
VAT (17½%)	119.70
AMOUNT DUE	803.70

PART ONE, TASK 1, CONTINUED

PURCHASE ORDER   **ORDER NO 724**

From: His 'n' Hers Fashions
             27-29 Riverside
             St Philips
             BRISTOL BS1 8SN
             Tel: 0117 9230460

To: *H I P Spinner*
             The Triangle, Clevedon
             North East Somerset
             BS21 7NT

Date of order: **7 March 20X1**   Date required:

Quantity	Ref No	Description	Unit Price £ p	Total Amount £ p
5	MW 54 50	Hopsack trousers, brown size 34	12.50	62.50
4	MW 57 76	Hopsack trousers, blue size 36	12.50	50.00
8	MW 43 05	Pleated cord trousers, grey size 32	14.00	112.00
10	MW 47 76	Pleated baggy trousers, black size 36	16.50	165.00
				389.50

Please quote order no on delivery note, invoice and other correspondence.

Signature *S McMahon*
....

authorised   date   *7/3/X1*
....

PART ONE, TASK 1, CONTINUED

PURCHASE ORDER   **ORDER NO 728**

From: His 'n' Hers Fashions
             27-29 Riverside
             St Philips
             BRISTOL BS1 8SN
             Tel: 0117 9230460

To: *I M Wilcox*
             4 New Road, Chippenham
             WILTS
             SN15 4DW

Date of order: **7 March 20X1**   Date required:

Quantity	Ref No	Description	Unit Price £ p	Total Amount £ p
4	LW 50 19	Mouflon jacket, jade size 12	32.00	128.00
8	LW 46 89	Pure wool duffle coat, purple size 10	40.00	320.00
3	LW 46 87	Pure wool duffle coat, forest green size 14	40.00	120.00
5	LW 40 80	Tweed wrapover coat, grey size 16	32.00	160.00
				728.00

Please quote order no on delivery note, invoice and other correspondence.

Signature   *S McMahon*
                 ....

authorised   date   *7/3/X1*
                 ....

PART ONE, TASK 1, CONTINUED

PURCHASE ORDER   **ORDER NO *730***

From: His 'n' Hers Fashions
              27-29 Riverside
              St Philips
              BRISTOL BS1 8SN
              Tel: 0117 9230460

To: *Look C Fashions*
              36 Fore Street
              Trowbridge
              Wilts BA14 8QF

Date of order: ***8 March 20X1***   Date required:

Quantity	Ref No	Description	Unit Price £ p	Total Amount £ p
5	LW 55 97	Jogging suit, royal blue size 10/12	9.00	45.00
5	LW 55 97	" " " " size 14/16	9.00	45.00
10	LW 55 99	Jogging suit, red size 10/12	9.00	90.00
20	LW 55 99	" " " size 14/16	9.00	180.00
15	LW 36 16	Ski pants, black size 12	12.00	180.00
15	LW 36 16	" " " size 14	12.00	180.00
				720.00

Please quote order no on delivery note, invoice and other correspondence.

Signature   *S McMahon*
....

authorised   date   ***8/3/X1***
....

PART ONE, TASK 1, CONTINUED

PURCHASE ORDER   **ORDER NO 732**

From: His 'n' Hers Fashions
         27-29 Riverside
         St Philips
         BRISTOL BS1 8SN
         Tel: 0117 9230460

To: *Rainbow Wholesalers*
         15 Union Street
         BRISTOL
         BS1 5BW

Date of order: **11 March 20X1**   Date required:

Quantity	Ref No	Description	Unit Price £ p	Total Amount £ p
8	LW 35 69	Stonewash jeans size 10	15.00	120.00
12	LW 35 69	" " " size 12	15.00	180.00
7	LW 35 69	" " " size 14	15.00	105.00
3	LW 35 69	" " " size 16	15.00	45.00
6	LW 36 27	Stretch cord jeans, grey size 10	12.00	72.00
8	LW 36 27	" " " " size 12	12.00	96.00
4	LW 36 27	" " " " size 14	12.00	48.00
				666.00

Please quote order no on delivery note, invoice and other correspondence.

Signature *S McMahon*
....

authorised   date   *11/3/X1*
....

PART ONE, TASK 1, CONTINUED

PURCHASE ORDER   **ORDER NO *734***

From: **His 'n' Hers Fashions**
             27-29 Riverside
             St Philips
             BRISTOL BS1 8SN
             Tel: 0117 9230460

To: *Saver and Spender*
             12 Rodney Walk
             Cheltenham
             GLOS GL50 6DX

Date of order: **11 March 20X1**   Date required:

Quantity	Ref No	Description	Unit Price £ p	Total Amount £ p
10	MW 70 60	Sweatshirt, blue size S	8.50	85.00
12	MW 70 60	" " size M	8.50	102.00
8	MW 70 60	" " size L	8.50	68.00
12	MW 15 52	Collarless shirt, white size S	8 75	105.00
14	MW 15 52	" " " size M	8.75	122.50
8	MW 15 52	" " " size L	8.75	70.00
				552.50

Please quote order no on delivery note, invoice and other correspondence.

Signature *S McMahon*
....

authorised   date   *11/3/X1*
                                            ....

PART ONE, TASK 1, CONTINUED

PURCHASE ORDER   ORDER NO *745*

From: His 'n' Hers Fashions
27-29 Riverside
St Philips
BRISTOL BS1 8SN
Tel: 0117 9230460

To: *Rainbow Wholesalers*
15 Union Street
BRISTOL
BS1 5BW

Date of order: **12 March 20X1**   Date required:

Quantity	Ref No	Description	Unit Price £ p	Total Amount £ p
8	MW 34 43	Bleached jeans, blue size 30	17.00	136.00
10	MW 34 43	" " " size 32	17.00	170.00
12	MW 34 43	" " " size 34	17.00	204.00
				510.00

Please quote order no on delivery note, invoice and other correspondence.

Signature *S McMahon*
....

authorised   date   *12/3/X1*
....

PART ONE, TASK 1, CONTINUED

PURCHASE ORDER   ORDER NO *748*

From: His 'n' Hers Fashions
                 27-29 Riverside
                 St Philips
                 BRISTOL BS1 8SN
                 Tel: 0117 9230460

To: *Look C Fashions*
                 36 Fore Street
                 Trowbridge
                 BA14 8QF

Date of order: **13 March 20X1**   Date required:

Quantity	Ref No	Description	Unit Price £ p	Total Amount £ p
12	LW 56 01	Jogging suit, black size 10/12	9.00	108.00
15	LW 56 01	" " " size 14/16	9.00	135.00
8	LW 56 00	Jogging suit, purple size 10/12	9.00	72.00
10	LW 56 00	" " " size 14/16	9.00	90.00
				405.00

Please quote order no on delivery note, invoice and other correspondence.

Signature *S McMahon*
....

authorised   date   *13/3/X1*
....

PART ONE, TASK 1, CONTINUED

GOODS RECEIVED NOTE

Date: *15 March 20X1*   NO *1098*

Order No *728*   Rec'd from   *I M Wilcox*

QUANTITY	DESCRIPTION
4	Mouflon jacket, jade size 12
8	Wool duffle coat, purple size 10
3	Wool duffle coat, green size 14
5	Tweed wrapover coat, grey size 16

RECEIVED IN GOOD CONDITION   *K Winslow*

....

GOODS RECEIVED NOTE

Date: *16 March 20X1*   NO *1099*

Order No *730*   Rec'd from   *Look C Fashions*

QUANTITY	DESCRIPTION
5	Jogging suit, royal blue size 10/12
5	" " " " size 14/16
10	" " red size 10/12
20	" " " size 14/16
15	Ski pants, black size 12
15	" " " size 14

RECEIVED IN GOOD CONDITION

....

PART ONE, TASK 1, CONTINUED

GOODS RECEIVED NOTE

Date: *16 March 20X1*

Order No 734

NO *1100*

Rec'd from *Saver and Spender*

QUANTITY	DESCRIPTION
10	Sweatshirt, blue size S
12	" " size M
8	" " size L
12	Collarless shirt, white size S
14	" " " " M
8	" " " " L

RECEIVED IN GOOD CONDITION   *K Winslow*

....

GOODS RECEIVED NOTE

Date: *16 March 20X1*

Order No 732

NO *1102*

Rec'd from *Rainbow Wholesalers*

QUANTITY	DESCRIPTION
8	Stonewash jeans size 10
12	" " " 12
7	" " " 14
3	" " " 16
6	Stretch cord jeans, grey size 10
8	" " " " " 12
4	" " " " " 14

RECEIVED IN GOOD CONDITION   *K Winslow*

....

PART ONE, TASK 1, CONTINUED

GOODS RECEIVED NOTE

Date: *18 March 20X1*

Order No 745

NO *1103*

Rec'd from *Rainbow Wholesalers*

QUANTITY	DESCRIPTION
8	Bleached jeans, blue size 30
10	" " " " 32
12	" " " " 34

RECEIVED IN GOOD CONDITION   *K Winslow*

....

GOODS RECEIVED NOTE

Date: *18 March 20X1*

Order No 724

NO *1106*

Rec'd from *H I P Spinner*

QUANTITY	DESCRIPTION
5	Hopsack trousers, brown size 34
4	" " blue " 36
8	Pleated cord trousers, grey size 32
10	Pleated baggy trousers, black size 36

RECEIVED IN GOOD CONDITION   *K Winslow*

....

PART ONE, TASK 1, CONTINUED

GOODS RECEIVED NOTE

Date: *19 March 20X1*   NO *1107*

Order No *748*   Rec'd from *Look C Fashions*

QUANTITY	DESCRIPTION
12	Jogging suit, black size 10/12
15	" " " size 14/16
8	Jogging suit, purple size 10/12
10	" " " size 14/16

RECEIVED IN GOOD CONDITION   *K Winslow*
....

PART TWO, TASK 4

PAYMENTS SCHEDULE

Supplier	Gross (before discount) £	VAT £	Net £
H I P Spinner 2% settlement discount to be taken	1,595.07	233.50	1,361.57
Look C Fashions 3% settlement discount to be taken	1,051.12	152.53	898.59

PART THREE, TASK 9

STATEMENT OF ACCOUNT

Look C Fashions
36 Fore Street
Trowbridge
Wilts BA14 8QF

Tel: 01225 78973
Fax: 01225 78986
VAT Reg No: 617 2394 408

Statement date: 28 March 20X1

To: His 'n' Hers Fashions
        27-29 Riverside
        St Philips
        BRISTOL BS1 8SN

Date	No	Details	Debit £	Debit p	Credit £	Credit p	Balance £	Balance p
25 Mar		Balance					2,124	16
27 Mar	01421	Invoice	803	70			2,927	86
27 Mar	01428	Invoice	452	08			3,379	94
						Amount now due	3,379	94

AAT UNIT 2

MOCK DEVOLVED ASSESSMENT 1

HIS 'N' HERS FASHIONS

ANSWER BOOKLET

ANSWERS - PART ONE, TASK 1

MEMORANDUM

TO

FROM

DATE

SUBJECT

ANSWERS – PART ONE, TASK 2

**His 'n' Hers Fashions
27-29 Riverside
St Philips
BRISTOL BS1 8SN
Telephone: 0117 9230460
Fax: 0117 9230462**

ANSWERS - PART ONE, TASK 3

PURCHASES DAY BOOK

Date	Details	Invoice No	Gross		VAT		Ladies Wear Net		Mens Wear Net	
20X1			£	p	£	p	£	p	£	p
	Totals									

ANSWERS - PART TWO, TASK 4

PAYMENTS WORKING SCHEDULE

ANSWERS - PART TWO, TASK 5

_____ Date	**Financial Bank Plc** 01 - 89 - 34
_____ Payee	Shepherd's Bush Green Branch **fb**
	352 Shepherd's Bush Green W12 6TH _____ 20

Pay _____ only

£ [   ]

HIS 'N' HERS FASHIONS

£ _____

000267

000267   01 - 89 - 34   47586909

	Date
	Payee
£	
000268	

Financial Bank Plc
Shepherd's Bush Green Branch
352 Shepherd's Bush Green W12 6TH

fb

01 - 89 - 34

_____ 20 ____

Pay _____ only

£ |_____|

HIS 'N' HERS FASHIONS

000268   01 - 89 - 34   47586909

ANSWERS - PART TWO, TASK 6

Cash Payments Book							
Date	Narrative	Cheque no	Total	Creditors	Salaries	VAT	Discount received

ANSWERS - PART THREE, TASK 7

SUBSIDIARY (PURCHASES) LEDGER

Dr				Account: *H I P Spinner*		Cr	
20X1		£	p	20X1		£	p
				25 - 3	*Balance b/d*	2,739 - 38	

Dr				Account: *I M Wilcox*		Cr	
20X1		£	p	20X1		£	p

Dr				Account: *Look C Fashions*		Cr	
20X1		£	p	20X1		£	p
				25-3	*Balance b/d*	2,124 - 16	

Dr				Account: *Saver and Spender*		Cr	
20X1		£	p	20X1		£	p
				25-3	*Balance b/d*	414 - 91	

ANSWERS - PART THREE, TASK 7, CONTINUED

SUBSIDIARY (PURCHASES) LEDGER

Dr				Account: *Rainbow Wholesalers*		Cr	
20X1		£	p	20X1		£	p
				25-3	*Balance b/d*	892	- 72

Dr				Account:		Cr	
20X1		£	p	20X1		£	p

Dr				Account:		Cr	
20X1		£	p	20X1		£	p

Dr				Account:		Cr	
20X1		£	p	20X1		£	p

ANSWERS - PART THREE, TASK 8

MAIN LEDGER

Dr				Account: *Purchase Ledger Control*		Cr	
20X1		£	p	20X1		£	p
				25-3	*Balance b/d*	6,171-17	

Dr				Account: *VAT*		Cr	
20X1		£	p	20X1		£	p
				25-3	*Balance b/d*	12,484-58	

Dr				Account: *Purchases - Menswear*		Cr	
20X1		£	p	20X1		£	p
25-3	*Balance b/d*	24,508-14					

Dr				Account: *Purchases - Ladieswear*		Cr	
20X1		£	p	20X1		£	p
25-3	*Balance b/d*	38,668-50					

Dr				Account: *Discounts Received*		Cr	
20X1		£	p	20X1		£	p

ANSWERS – PART THREE, TASK 9

SUPPLIER STATEMENT RECONCILIATION AS AT 29 MARCH 20X1

ANSWERS - PART THREE, TASK 9, CONTINUED

MEMORANDUM

AAT UNIT 2

MOCK DEVOLVED ASSESSMENT 2

SEAMER RETAIL LTD

QUESTIONS

DATA AND TASKS

Instructions

This simulation is designed to test your ability to make and record payments.

The situation is provided on the next page.

The simulation is divided into three parts as follows:

Part one: Petty cash

Task 1   Authorisation of petty cash claims

Task 2   Entries in petty cash book

Task 3   Reconciliation of cash box contents with petty cash book balance

Part two: Cash Payments

Task 4   Preparing cheques and remittance advices

Task 5   Entering cheques in cash book

Part three: Writing up ledger

Task 6   Posting from cash book and petty cash book to ledger accounts

Task 7   Drafting memo

Note that the final task referred to above will require you to explain any discrepancies you have encountered in the course of the simulation; you are advised to make a brief note of such discrepancies as you come across them by way of reminder.

This booklet also contains a large amount of data which you will need to complete the tasks and you are advised to read the whole of the simulation before commencing as all of the information may be of value and is not necessarily supplied in the sequence in which you might wish to deal with it.

Your answers should be set out in the answer booklet using the specimen forms provided.

You are allowed **three hours** to complete your work.

A high level of accuracy is required. Check your work carefully before handing it in.

Correcting fluid should not be used. Errors should be crossed out neatly and clearly. You should write in black ink, not pencil.

THE SITUATION

Your name is A Student and you work for Seamer Retail Limited, 37 Cain Road, Scarborough YO12 4HF. Seamer is a retailer of gardening and DIY (do-it-yourself) supplies. Your duties involve both bookkeeping and, occasionally, acting as a cash supervisor in the retail area of the company's premises. The transactions you are required to deal with take place in the week ending Friday 7 November 20X1.

Petty cash

Petty cash is maintained on an imprest system, with a float of £100 replenished at the end of each accounting week. When staff incur petty cash expenditure they complete a voucher (which must be supported by a receipt) and then submit it to you. Provided the amount is not above £10, you authorise the expenditure yourself by signing and dating the petty cash voucher and then pay the cash. For amounts above £10, authorisation is required by the Accountant.

Expenditure

Another of your duties is to make out cheques to pay suppliers. You are not an authorised signatory of the company bank account: once you have prepared the cheques, they are passed for signing to Gillian Russell, the company accountant.

It is Gillian Russell who decides when invoices should be paid. She prepares a list each week, which is passed to you for the preparation of appropriate remittance advices and cheques. When preparing cheques to suppliers who offer settlement discounts, it is your responsibility to ensure that advantage is taken of any discounts available.

PART ONE

TASK 1

Refer to the petty cash receipts given. The related petty cash vouchers are given in the answer booklet. For each claim that you are satisfied with you are required to complete the relevant voucher ready for entering in the petty cash book. The vouchers are to be numbered in sequence, beginning with number 175.

In the case of any claim you do not feel able to process, explain what action you would take. Use the form given in the answer booklet.

(Note: In the final task of this simulation you will be required to write a memo to the Accountant setting out any discrepancies of which she should be aware, including any you discover in this task.)

TASK 2

The petty cash book for Seamer Retail is given in the answer booklet. You are required to enter in it the petty cash vouchers that you have processed in task 1 above, and then to total and balance off the petty cash book for the week ended 7 November 20X1, including the entries necessary to restore the imprest.

TASK 3

The contents of the petty cash box at close of business on 7 November 20X1 are listed below. You are required to reconcile the total of cash on hand with the balance shown in the petty cash book. Use the blank in the answer booklet to set out your reconciliation.

Contents of petty cash box

£10 notes   ×   4
£5 notes   ×   3
£1 coins   ×   6
50p coins   ×   3
20p coins   ×   4
10p coins   ×   9
2p coins   ×   8
1p coins   ×   11

PART TWO

TASK 4

The Accountant has informed you that the following invoices can now be paid.

Supplier	Invoice number	Invoice date	Amount Goods (ex VAT) £	VAT £	Terms
Baxley Limited Station Road Horsford TV12 3EW	4132	26/10/X1	1,788.56	309.86	1% cash discount for settlement within 10 days
Harborne Limited 12 Barton Street Apton AN3 4RT	2541	7/10/X1	2,076.22	363.33	Net 30 days
Hurley Limited 241 Steels Avenue Picton SR5 9TY	1008	1/10/X1	300.17	52.52	Net 30 days
Allen and Banks 49 Exley Road Traxham TM5 1UJ	1673	27/10/X1	654.08	112.74	1.5% cash discount for settlement within 14 days
Wallace Limited 101-105 Knighton Rd Brixley BY2 3FR	4321	10/10/X1	102.66	17.96	Net 30 days

You are required to complete cheques ready for signature by Gillian Russell in respect of each of these invoices. You should ensure in each case that any discount to which the company is entitled is accounted for in calculating the amount of the cheques (the cheques will be posted on 7 November 20X1). You are also required to complete remittance advices.

Blank cheques and remittance advices are provided in the answer booklet.

TASK 5

An extract from the company's cash book (payments side) appears in the answer booklet. You are required to enter in the book all of the cheques prepared in task 4, and also the petty cash imprest cheque (cheque no 305081) calculated earlier in task 2. Total all of the cash book columns.

PART THREE

TASK 6

In the answer booklet certain main ledger and subsidiary (purchases) ledger accounts have been extracted from the books of Seamer Retail Limited.

You are required to make the following postings to these ledger accounts.

(a) Post from the cash book (payments side) for the week ended 7 November 20X1 to the appropriate main ledger accounts.

(b) Post from the cash book (payments side) for the week ended 7 November 20X1 to the appropriate subsidiary (purchases) ledger accounts.

(c) Post from the petty cash book for the week ended 7 November 20X1 to the appropriate main ledger accounts.

TASK 7

You are required to write a memo to Gillian Russell, the Accountant, explaining any discrepancies you encountered in the course of the tasks above. Use the blank memo form in the answer booklet.

```
Stationery Supplies
Hill Street, Scarborough
Telephone 01723 23478

3 November 20X1

Goods                   13.07

VAT                      2.28

Total                   15.35

Amount tendered         20.00

Change                   4.65

Vat registration no:245 9162 47
```

```
Stationery Supplies
Hill Street, Scarborough
Telephone 01723 23478

4 November 20X1

Goods                    9.45

VAT                      1.65

Total                   11.10

Amount tendered         15.00

Change                   3.90

Vat registration no:245 9162 47
```

```
Stationery Supplies
Hill Street, Scarborough
Telephone 01723 23478

5 November 20X1

Goods                    6.24

VAT                      1.09

Total                    7.33

Amount tendered         10.00

Change                   2.67

Vat registration no:245 9162 47
```

```
Stationery Supplies
Hill Street, Scarborough
Telephone 01723 23478

7 November 20X1

Goods                    5.92

VAT                      1.03

Total                    6.95

Amount tendered         10.00

Change                   3.05

Vat registration no:245 9162 47
```

```
Ace Taxis
Telephone 01723 29865

Date    4 November 20X1

Received with thanks   £5 - 20


Vat registration no: 337 8714 29
```

```
Ace Taxis
Telephone 01723 29865

Date    7 November 20X1

Received with thanks   £6 - 10


Vat registration no: 337 8714 29
```

POST OFFICE		P325		
Order for stamps, etc				
*This is **not** a certificate of posting*				
Postage stamps		Miscellaneous		
	£			£
Stamps	5-25			
		B/F FROM COLUMN 1		
		GRAND TOTAL		5-25
TOTAL COLUMN 1		*4 November 20X1*		

POST OFFICE		P325		
Order for stamps, etc				
*This is **not** a certificate of posting*				
Postage stamps		Miscellaneous		
	£			£
Stamps	0-76			
		B/F FROM COLUMN 1		
		GRAND TOTAL		0-76
TOTAL COLUMN 1		*4 November 20X1*		

POST OFFICE		P325		
Order for stamps, etc				
*This is **not** a certificate of posting*				
Postage stamps		Miscellaneous		
	£			£
Stamps	3-94			
		B/F FROM COLUMN 1		
		GRAND TOTAL		3-94
TOTAL COLUMN 1		*6 November 20X1*		

POST OFFICE		P325		
Order for stamps, etc				
*This is **not** a certificate of posting*				
Postage stamps		Miscellaneous		
	£			£
Stamps	12-35			
		B/F FROM COLUMN 1		
		GRAND TOTAL		12-35
TOTAL COLUMN 1		*7 November 20X1*		

216

AAT UNIT 2

MOCK DEVOLVED ASSESSMENT 2

SEAMER RETAIL LTD

ANSWER BOOKLET

ANSWERS - PART ONE, TASK 1

Petty Cash Voucher	Folio _____ Date _____		
	AMOUNT		
For what required	£		p
Stationery	11		10
	11		10
Signature	*Adam Haynes*		
Passed by			

Petty Cash Voucher	Folio _____ Date _____		
	AMOUNT		
For what required	£		p
Stationery	6		95
	6		95
Signature	*Adam Haynes*		
Passed by			

Petty Cash Voucher	Folio _____ Date _____		
	AMOUNT		
For what required	£		p
Stationery	4		94
	4		94
Signature	*Adam Haynes*		
Passed by			

Petty Cash Voucher	Folio _____ Date _____		
	AMOUNT		
For what required	£		p
Stationery	7		33
	7		33
Signature	*Adam Haynes*		
Passed by			

Petty Cash Voucher	Folio _____ Date _____		
	AMOUNT		
For what required	£		p
Stationery	15		35
	15		35
Signature	*Adam Haynes*		
Passed by			

Petty Cash Voucher	Folio _____ Date _____		
	AMOUNT		
For what required	£		p
Stamps	12		35
	12		35
Signature	*Jane Hawkins*		
Passed by			

ANSWERS - PART ONE, TASK 1, CONTINUED

Petty Cash Voucher	Folio _____ Date _____		
		AMOUNT	
For what required		£	p
Stamps		5	25
		5	25
Signature	*Jane Hawkins*		
Passed by			

Petty Cash Voucher	Folio _____ Date _____		
		AMOUNT	
For what required		£	p
Stamps		3	94
		3	94
Signature	*Jane Hawkins*		
Passed by			

Petty Cash Voucher	Folio _____ Date _____		
		AMOUNT	
For what required		£	p
Stamps		0	76
		0	76
Signature	*Jane Hawkins*		
Passed by			

Petty Cash Voucher	Folio _____ Date _____		
		AMOUNT	
For what required		£	p
Taxi fare (meeting with auditors)		5	20
		5	20
Signature	*Gillian Russell*		
Passed by			

Petty Cash Voucher	Folio _____ Date _____		
		AMOUNT	
For what required		£	p
Taxi fare (meeting with supplier)		6	10
		6	10
Signature	*Ben Thornley*		
Passed by			

ANSWERS - PART ONE, TASK 1, CONTINUED

MEMORANDUM OF DISCREPANCIES

FOR LETTER TO GILLIAN RUSSELL

Details of claim	Action

ANSWERS - PART ONE, TASK 2

PETTY CASH BOOK

								PCB22
Receipts	*Date*	*Details*	*Voucher*	*Total*	*VAT*	*Travel*	*Stationery*	*Postage*
£	20X1			£	£	£	£	£
100 00	31-Oct	Balance b/d						

ANSWERS - PART ONE, TASK 3

RECONCILIATION OF PETTY CASH

Petty Cash Book

	£
Opening balance of imprest	
Payments	
	───────
Closing balance	
Cash counted	───────
	═══════

ANSWERS - PART TWO, TASK 4

REMITTANCE ADVICE

From: **Seamer Retail Limited**
             37 Cain Road
             Scarborough
             YO12 4HF
To:

Date:

Details	Amount	
	£	p
Cheque no enclosed		

In case of query, please contact

_____ Date
_____ Payee
_____
_____
_____
_____
£ _____
305082

Wadsworth Bank Plc   25-46-70
Chambers Street, Scarborough YO12 3NZ

_____ 20 ___

Pay _____ only

£ |_____|

For Seamer Retail Ltd

305082   25-46-70   21758391

ANSWERS - PART TWO, TASK 4, CONTINUED

REMITTANCE ADVICE

From: **Seamer Retail Limited**
37 Cain Road
Scarborough
YO12 4HF

To:

Date:

Details	Amount	
	£	p
Cheque no enclosed		

In case of query, please contact

_____ Date

_____ Payee

_____

_____

_____

_____

£ _____

305083

Wadsworth Bank Plc   25-46-70
Chambers Street, Scarborough YO12 3NZ

_____ 20 ___

Pay _____ only

£ _____

For Seamer Retail Ltd

305083   25-46-70   21758391

ANSWERS - PART TWO, TASK 4, CONTINUED

REMITTANCE ADVICE

From: **Seamer Retail Limited**
           37 Cain Road
           Scarborough
           YO12 4HF

To:

Date:

Details	Amount	
	£	p
Cheque no enclosed		

In case of query, please contact

_____ Date	**Wadsworth Bank Plc** 25-46-70
_____ Payee	Chambers Street, Scarborough YO12 3NZ

_____ Date

_____ Payee

_____

_____

_____

_____

£ _____

305084

Wadsworth Bank Plc   25-46-70
Chambers Street, Scarborough YO12 3NZ

_____ 20 _____

Pay _____ only

£ [ ]

For Seamer Retail Ltd

305084   25-46-70   21758391

ANSWERS - PART TWO, TASK 4, CONTINUED

REMITTANCE ADVICE

From: **Seamer Retail Limited**
        37 Cain Road
        Scarborough
        YO12 4HF

To:

Date:

Details	Amount	
	£	p
Cheque no enclosed		

In case of query, please contact

_____ Date			
_____ Payee			

Wadsworth Bank Plc   25-46-70
Chambers Street, Scarborough YO12 3NZ

                                                 _____ 20 ___

Pay   only   £

£ _____

                                             For Seamer Retail Ltd

305085   305085   25-46-70   21758391

ANSWERS (PART TWO, TASK 4, CONTINUED)

REMITTANCE ADVICE

From: **Seamer Retail Limited**
37 Cain Road
Scarborough
YO12 4HF

To:

Date:

Details	Amount £	p
Cheque no enclosed		

In case of query, please contact

_____ Date

_____ Payee

_____

_____

_____

_____

£ _____

305086

Wadsworth Bank Plc   25-46-70
Chambers Street, Scarborough YO12 3NZ

_____ 20 ___

Pay _____ only

£ [   ]

For Seamer Retail Ltd

_____

305086   25-46-70   21758391

ANSWERS – PART TWO, TASK 5

CASH BOOK PAYMENTS

							CPB 53
Date	Payee/details	Cheque no	Total	VAT	Creditors	Discount Received	Sundry
20X1			£	£	£	£	£

ANSWERS - PART THREE, TASK 6

MAIN LEDGER

Account *Postage*

Date 20X1	Details	Amount £	Date 20X1	Details	Amount £
			Credit		
31-Oct	Bal b/f	213.76			

Account *Stationery*

Date 20X1	Details	Amount £	Date 20X1	Details	Amount £
			Credit		
31-Oct	Bal b/f	543.09			

Account *Travel*

Date 20X1	Details	Amount £	Date 20X1	Details	Amount £
			Credit		
31-Oct	Bal b/f	513.88			

ANSWERS - PART THREE, TASK 6, CONTINUED

MAIN LEDGER

Account *Purchase ledger control*

Date 20X1	Details	Amount £	Date 20X1	Details	Amount £
			31-Oct	Bal b/f	28,996.21

Debit — Credit

Account *VAT*

Date 20X1	Details	Amount £	Date 20X1	Details	Amount £
			31-Oct	Bal b/f	2,499.04

Debit — Credit

Account *Cash sales*

Date 20X1	Details	Amount £	Date 20X1	Details	Amount £
			31-Oct	Bal b/f	51,235.99

Debit — Credit

ANSWERS - PART THREE, TASK 6, CONTINUED

MAIN LEDGER

Account	*Discount received*				
Debit			Credit		
Date 20X1	Details	Amount £	Date 20X1	Details	Amount £
			31-Oct	Bal b/f	147.39

ANSWERS - PART THREE, TASK 6, CONTINUED

SUBSIDIARY (PURCHASES) LEDGER

Account *Allen and Banks*

Date 20X1	Details	Amount £	Date 20X1	Details	Amount £
			31-Oct	Bal b/f	1,152.90

Account *Baxley Limited*

Date 20X1	Details	Amount £	Date 20X1	Details	Amount £
			31-Oct	Bal b/f	3,012.75

Account *Harborne Limited*

Date 20X1	Details	Amount £	Date 20X1	Details	Amount £
			31-Oct	Bal b/f	3,225.67

ANSWERS - PART THREE, TASK 6, CONTINUED

SUBSIDIARY (PURCHASES) LEDGER

Account *Hurley Limited*

Debit			Credit		
Date 20X1	Details	Amount £	Date 20X1	Details	Amount £
			31-Oct	Bal b/f	961.44

Account *Wallace Limited*

Debit			Credit		
Date 20X1	Details	Amount £	Date 20X1	Details	Amount £
			31-Oct	Bal b/f	546.08

ANSWERS - PART THREE, TASK 7

MEMO

To:

From:

Subject:

Date:

AAT UNIT 2

ANSWERS

KEY TECHNIQUES – ANSWERS

Credit purchases: documents

1

Invoice from A J Broom & Company Ltd

-   7 joist hangers were invoiced and delivered but only 5 were ordered.

Invoice from Jenson Ltd

-   the VAT calculation is incorrect – the amount should be £99.37.

Invoice from Haddow Bros

-   12 sheets were invoiced and ordered but only 10 were delivered.

2

Credit note from J M Bond & Co

-   the trade discount deducted should have been £6.16. Therefore, the total amount of credit is wrong.

Credit purchases: primary records

1

Purchases day book								
Date	Invoice no	Code	Supplier	Total	VAT	Wood	Bricks/ cement	Consumables
3/5/X1	077401	PL16	Magnum Supplies	493 90	72 30		421 60	
	046193	PL08	A J Broom & Co Ltd	118 47	17 64	85 08		15 75
	47823	PL13	Jenson Ltd	433 74	62 94	284 80	86 00	
				1,046 11	152 88	369 88	507 60	15 75

2

Purchases day book								
Date	Invoice no	Code	Supplier	Total	VAT	Paint	Wallpaper	Other
22/3/X1	047992	PL03	Mortimer & Co	180 97	26 37		112 00	42 60
	61624	PL06	F L Decor Supplies	64 29	9 57		54 72	
	05531	PL08	Specialist Paint Ltd	219 11	32 21	98 40		88 50
				464 37	68 15	98 40	166 72	131 10

3

Purchases returns day book								
Date	Credit note no	Code	Supplier	Total	VAT	Wood	Bricks/ cement	Consumables
3/5/X1	CN06113	PL13	Jenson Ltd	30 07	4 36	25 71		
	06132	PL03	Haddow Bros	41 70	6 10	35 60		
	C4163	PL16	Magnum Supplies	45 80	6 70		39 10	
				117 57	17 16	61 31	39 10	-

4

Purchases day book								
Date	Invoice no	Code	Supplier	Total	VAT	Fabric	Header tape	Other
12/4/X1	06738	PL03	Fabric Supplies Ltd	1,097 22	160 62	798 00	138 60	
	0328	PL04	Lillian Fisher	107 74	16 04			91 70
	CN0477	PL05	Headstream & Co	(79 90)	(11 90)	(51 40)	(16 60)	
	07359	PL01	Mainstream Fabrics	330 04	48 52	281 52		
				1,455 10	213 28	1,028 12	122 00	91 70

Credit purchases: accounting

1

Main ledger

Creditors control account

	£			£
		1 May	Balance b/d	3,104.67
		5 May	PDB	1,002.57

VAT account

	£			£
5 May PDB	149.30	1 May	Balance b/d	723.56

Purchases account

	£		£
1 May Balance b/d	24,367.48		
5 May PDB	853.27		

Subsidiary ledger

T Ives   PL01

	£			£
		1 May	Balance b/d	332.56
		5 May	PDB 002633	192.98

H Samuels   PL02

	£			£
		1 May	Balance b/d	286.90
		3 May	PDB 92544	109.79

L Jameson   PL03

	£			£
		1 May	Balance b/d	623.89
		1 May	PDB 36558	393.91

G Rails   PL04

	£			£
		1 May	Balance b/d	68.97
		4 May	PDB 03542	180.93

K Davison   PL07

	£			£
		1 May	Balance b/d	125.47
		1 May	PDB 102785	124.96

2

Main ledger

Creditors control account

	£			£
		17/2	Balance b/d	2,357.57
		24/2	PDB	942.08

VAT account

		£			£
24/2	PDB	140.30	17/2	Balance b/d	662.47

Purchases – 01 account

		£		£
17/2	Balance b/d	14,275.09		
24/2	PDB	222.05		

Purchases – 02 account

		£		£
17/2	Balance b/d	12,574 26		
24/2	PDB	179.04		

Purchases – 03 account

		£		£
17/2	Balance b/d	29,384.74		
24/2	PDB	302.55		

Purchases – 04 account

		£		£
17/2	Balance b/d	9,274.36		
24/2	PDB	98.14		

Subsidiary ledger

P & F Davis & Co PL03

		£			£
			17/2	Balance b/d	368.36
			21/2	PDB 46120	166.54
			24/2	PDB 46122	189.23

Clooney & Partner PL06

		£			£
			17/2	Balance b/d	226.48
			22/2	PDB 46121	230.58

S Doorman PL07

		£			£
23/2	PDB CN463	21.51	17/2	Balance b/d	218.47
			20/2	PDB 46119	189.53

Fred Janitor PL11

		£			£
23/2	PDB CN462	30.99	17/2	Balance b/d	111.45
			20/2	PDB 46118	218.70

3

JOURNAL ENTRY		No: 0254	
Prepared by: A N OTHER			
Authorised by:			
Date: 12/3/X1			
Narrative:			
To post the purchases day book to the main ledger			
Account		*Debit*	*Credit*
VAT		184.77	
Purchases – 01		310.76	
Purchases – 02		156.09 ·	
Purchases – 03		245.66	
Purchases – 04		343.43	
Creditors control			1,240.71
TOTALS		1,240.71	1,240.71

Subsidiary ledger

ABG Ltd PL02

		£			£
12/3	PDB CN477	48.31	5/3	Balance b/d	486.90
			10/3	PDB 016127	292.58

Forker & Co PL07

		£			£
10/3	PDB C4366	23.73	5/3	Balance b/d	503.78
			8/3	PDB 11675	207.24

Print Associates PL08

		£			£
			5/3	Balance b/d	229.56
			9/3	PDB 46251	230.04

Homer Ltd   PL12

	£			£
		5/3	Balance b/d	734.90
		8/3	PDB 06121	223.87
		11/3	PDB 06132	189.33

G Greg   PL19

	£			£
		5/3	Balance b/d	67.89
		11/3	PDB 77918	169.69

4

Main ledger

Creditors control account

		£			£
19/4	PRDB	245.10	12/4	Balance b/f	12,678.57

VAT account

	£			£
		12/4	Balance b/f	1,023.90
		19/4	PRDB	36.50

Purchases returns – 01 account

	£			£
		12/4	Balance b/f	337.60
		19/4	PRDB	60.40

Purchases returns – 02 account

	£			£
		12/4	Balance b/f	228.59
		19/4	PRDB	23.40

Purchases returns – 03 account

	£			£
		12/4	Balance b/f	889.46
		19/4	PRDB	108.00

Purchases returns – 04 account

	£			£
		12/4	Balance b/f	362.78
		19/4	PRDB	16 80

Subsidiary ledger

F Williams   *PL06*

		£			£
18/4	PRDB C4772	164.50	12/4	Balance b/f	673.47

K Bartlett   *PL13*

		£			£
19/4	PRDB 06638	53.11	12/4	Balance b/f	421.36

J D Withers   *PL16*

		£			£
15/4	PRDB C0179	27.49	12/4	Balance b/f	446.37

Making payments

1

REMITTANCE ADVICE

To:	Building Contract Supplies	NETHAN BUILDERS
	Unit 15	Brecon House
	Royal Estate	Stamford Road
	Manchester	Manchester
	M13 2EF	M16 4PL

Tel:	0161 521 6411
Fax:	0161 521 6412
VAT Reg no:	471 3860 42
Date:	18 May 20X1

Date	Invoice no	Amount £	Discount taken £	Paid £
18 May 20X1	07742	199.47	2.55	196.92

Total paid	£ 196 92
Cheque no	200550

REMITTANCE ADVICE

To:	Jenson Ltd 30 Longfield Park Kingsway M45 2TP	NETHAN BUILDERS Brecon House Stamford Road Manchester M16 4PL

Tel: 0161 521 6411
Fax: 0161 521 6412
VAT Reg no: 471 3860 42
Date: 18 May 20X1

Date	Invoice no	Amount £	Discount taken £	Paid £
18 May 20X1	47811	180.46	-	180.46

Total paid   £ 180 46

Cheque no   200551

REMITTANCE ADVICE

To:	Magnum Supplies 140/150 Park Estate Manchester M20 6EG

NETHAN BUILDERS
Brecon House
Stamford Road
Manchester
M16 4PL

Tel:	0161 521 6411
Fax:	0161 521 6412
VAT Reg no:	471 3860 42
Date:	18 May 20X1

Date	Invoice no	Amount £	Discount taken £	Paid £
18 May 20X1	077422	740.85	12.65	782.20

Total paid £ 728 20

Cheque no 200552

REMITTANCE ADVICE

To:	Haddow Bros The White House Standing Way Manchester M13 6FH	NETHAN BUILDERS Brecon House Stamford Road Manchester M16 4PL

Tel:	0161 521 6411
Fax:	0161 521 6412
VAT Reg no:	471 3860 42
Date:	18 May 20X1

Date	Invoice no	Amount £	Discount taken £	Paid £
18 May 20X1	G33940	500.46	–	500.46

Total paid   £ 500 46

Cheque no

200553

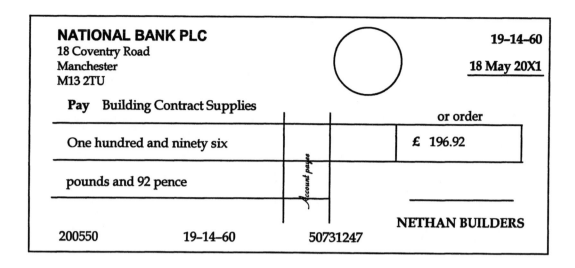

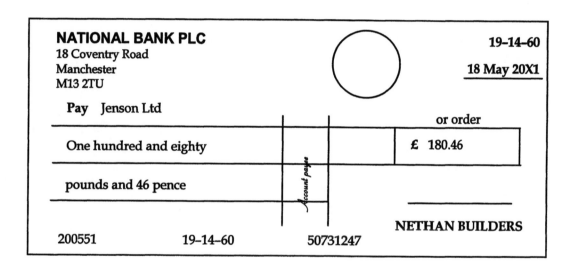

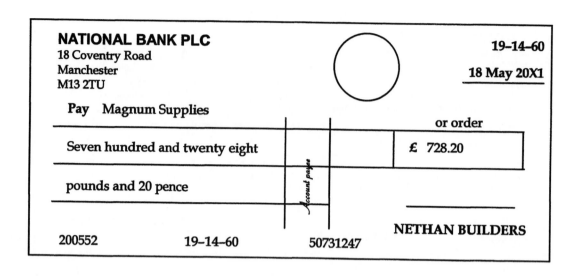

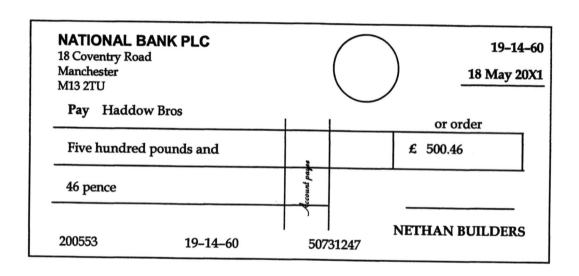

Accounting for payments

1

Cash payments book

Date	Details	Cheque no	Code	Total £	VAT £	Creditors ledger £	Cash purchases £	Other £	Discounts received £
20X1									
30/5	J M Bond	200572	PL01	247 56		247 56			
	Magnum Supplies	200573	PL16	662 36		662 36			13 25
	A J Broom	200574	PL08	153 57		153 57			
	Jenson Ltd	200575	PL13	336 57		336 57			6 73
	KKL Traders	200576	PL20	442 78		442.78			8 85
	Purchases	200577		108 66	16 18		92.48		
				1,951 50	16 18	1,842 84	92.48	-	28 83

Main ledger

Creditors control account

	£		£
30 May CPB	1,842.84	23 May Balance b/d	5,328.46
30 May CPB – discount	28.83		

VAT account

	£		£
30 May CPB	16.18	23 May Balance b/d	1,365.35

Purchases account

	£		£
23 May Balance b/d	36,785.90		
30 May CPB	92.48		

Discount received account

	£		£
		23 May Balance b/d	1,573.56
		30 May CPB	28.83

Subsidiary ledger

J M Bond   PL01

	£			£
30 May CPB 200572	247.56		23 May Balance b/d	247.56

A J Broom Ltd   PL08

	£			£
30 May CPB 200574	153.57		23 May Balance b/d	524.36

Jenson Ltd   PL13

	£			£
30 May CPB 200575	336.57		23 May Balance b/d	512.36
30 May CPB – discount	6.73			

Magnum Supplies   PL16

	£			£
30 May CPB 200573	662.36		23 May Balance b/d	675.61
30 May CPB – discount	13.25			

KKL Traders   PL20

	£			£
30 May CPB 200576	442.78		23 May Balance b/d	612.46
30 May CPB – discount	8.85			

2

Cash payments book

Date	Details	Cheque no	Code	Total £	VAT £	Creditors ledger £	Cash purchases £	Other £	Discounts received £
8 May	G Rails	001221	PL04	177 56		177 56			4 43
	L Jameson	001222	PL03	257 68		257 68			7 73
	Purchases	001223		216 43	32 23		184 20		
	K Davison	001224	PL07	167 89		167 89			
	T Ives	001225	PL01	289 06		289 06			5 79
	Purchases	001226		263 78	39 28		224 50		
	H Samuels	001227	PL02	124 36		124 36			
				1,496 76	71 51	1,016 55	408 70	-	17 95

JOURNAL ENTRY		No: 1468
Prepared by: A N OTHER		
Authorised by:		
Date: 8 May 20X1		
Narrative:		
To post the cash payments book for the week ending 8 May 20X1		
Account	*Debit*	*Credit*
Creditors control	1,016.55	
VAT	71.51	
Purchases	408.70	
Bank		1,496.76
Creditors control	17.95	
Discount received		17.95
TOTALS	1,514.71	1,514.71

Subsidiary ledger

		£			£
8 May	CPB 001225	289.06	1 May Balance b/d		332.56
8 May	CPB – discount	5.79			

T Ives — *PL01*

		£			£
8 May	CPB 001227	124.36	1 May Balance b/d		286.90

H Samuels — *PL02*

		£			£
8 May	CPB 001222	257.68	1 May Balance b/d		623.89
8 May	CPB – discount	7.73			

L Jameson — *PL03*

		£			£
8 May	CPB 001221	177.56	1 May Balance b/d		181.99
8 May	CPB – discount	4.43			

G Rails — *PL04*

		£			£
8 May	CPB 001224	167.89	1 May Balance b/d		167.89

K Davison — *PL07*

3

Cash payments book

Date	Details	Cheque no	Code	Total £	VAT £	Creditors ledger £	Cash purchases £	Other £	Discounts received £
12/3/X1	Homer Ltd	03648	PL12	168 70		168 70			5 06
	Forker & Co	03649	PL07	179 45		179 45			5 38
	Purchases	03650		334 87	49 87		285 00		
	Print Ass	03651	PL08	190 45		190 45			
	ABG Ltd	03652	PL02	220 67		220 67			6 62
	Purchases	03653		193 87	28 87		165 00		
	G Greg	03654	PL19	67 89		67 89			
				1,355 90	78 74	827 16	450 00	-	17 06

Main ledger

Creditors control account

		£			£
12/3	CPB	827.16	5/3	Balance b/d	4,136.24
12/3	CPB – discount	17.06			

VAT account

		£			£
12/3	CPB	78.74	5/3	Balance b/d	1,372.56

Purchases account

		£			£
5/3	Balance b/d	20,465.88			
12/3	CPB	450.00			

Discounts received account

		£			£
			5/3	Balance b/d	784 56
			12/3	CPB	17.06

Subsidiary ledger

ABG Ltd PL02

		£			£
12/3	CPB 03652	220.67	5/3	Balance b/d	486.90
12/3	CPB – discount	6.62			

Forker & Co PL07

		£			£
12/3	CPB 03649	179.45	5/3	Balance b/d	503.78
12/3	CPB – discount	5.38			

Print Associates PL08

		£			£
12/3	CPB 03651	190.45	5/3	Balance b/d	229.56

Homer Ltd PL12

		£			£
12/3	CPB 03648	168.70	5/3	Balance b/d	734.90
12/3	CPB – discount	5.06			

G Greg PL19

		£			£
12/3	CPB 03654	67.89	5/3	Balance b/d	67.89

Petty cash systems

1

Claimed by	Amount	Comment
J Athersych	£7.04	Valid
J Athersych	£4 85	Valid – less than £5
F Rivers	£12.80	Valid – authorised by department head
M Patterson	£6.60	Cannot be paid – no receipt
D R Ray	£42.80	Cannot be paid – more than £30
J Athersych	£3.70	Valid – less than £5
D R Ray	£12.50	Cannot be paid – not authorised by department head
M Patterson	£19.50	Valid
M T Noble	£17 46	Valid
J Norman	£7.60	Cannot be paid – not authorised by department head

2

Petty cash book											
Receipts			**Payments**								
Date	Narrative	Total £	Date	Narrative	Voucher no	Total £	Postage £	Stationery £	Tea & coffee £	Travel £	VAT £
	Bal b/d	100 00	30/4/X1	Coffee/milk	2534	4 68			4 68		
				Postage	2535	13 26	13 26				
				Stationery	2536	10 27		8 74			1 53
				Taxi fare	2537	15 00				12.77	2 23
				Postage	2538	6 75	6 75				
				Train fare	2539	7 40				7 40	
				Stationery	2540	3 86		3 29			0 57
						61 22	20 01	12 03	4 68	20 17	4 33

Main ledger accounts

Postage account

	£		£
23 Apr Balance b/d	231.67		
30 Apr PCB	20 01		

Stationery account

	£		£
23 Apr Balance b/d	334.78		
30 Apr PCB	12.03		

Tea and coffee account

	£		£
23 Apr Balance b/d	55.36		
30 Apr PCB	4.68		

Travel expenses account

	£		£
23 Apr Balance b/d	579.03		
30 Apr PCB	20.17		

VAT account

	£		£
30 Apr PCB	4.33	23 Apr Balance b/d	967.44

3

Petty cash book											
Receipts			**Payments**								
Date	Narrative	Total £	Date	Narrative	Voucher no	Total £	Postage £	Staff welfare £	Stationery £	Travel expenses £	VAT £
5/1/X1	Bal b/d	150 00	12/1/X1	Postage	03526	13 68	13 68				
				Staff welfare	03527	25 00		25 00			
				Stationery	03528	14 80			12 60		2 20
				Taxi fare	03529	12 00				10 21	1 79
				Staff welfare	03530	6 40		6 40			
				Postage	03531	12 57	12 57				
				Rail fare	03532	6 80				6 80	
				Stationery	03533	7 99			6 80		1.19
				Taxi fare	03534	18 80				16 00	2 80
						118 04	26 25	31 40	19 40	33 01	7 98

CHEQUE REQUISITION FORM

CHEQUE DETAILS

Date .... 12/1/X1 ....

Payee .... Cash ....

Amount   £   118.04 ....

Reason .. To restore petty cash ....

Invoice no (attached/to follow) - ....

Receipt (attached/to follow) - ....

Required by   (Print) .... PETTY CASHIER ....

                (Signature) .... Petty Cashier ....

Authorised by: ....

Main ledger accounts

Postage account

		£		£
5 Jan	Balance b/d	248.68		
12 Jan	PCB	26.25		

Staff welfare account

		£		£
5 Jan	Balance b/d	225.47		
12 Jan	PCB	31.40		

Stationery account

		£		£
5 Jan	Balance b/d	176.57		
12 Jan	PCB	19.40		

Travel expenses account

		£		£
5 Jan	Balance b/d	160.90		
12 Jan	PCB	33.01		

VAT account

		£			£
12 Jan	PCB	7.98	5 Jan	Balance b/d	2,385.78

4

Voucher total

	£
02634	13.73
02635	8.91
02636	10.57
02637	3.21
02638	11.30
02639	14.66
	62.38

Cash total

		£
£10 note	1	10.00
£5 note	2	10.00
£2 coin	3	6.00
£1 coin	7	7.00
50p coin	5	2.50
20p coin	4	0.80
10p coin	1	0.10
5p coin	2	0.10
2p coin	3	0.06
1p coin	6	0.06
		36.62

Reconciliation of cash and vouchers at 22 May 20X1

	£
Voucher total	62.38
Cash total	36.62
	99.00

The reconciliation shows that there is £1 missing. More cash has been paid out of the petty cash box than is supported by the petty cash vouchers. This could be due to a number of reasons:

♦ A petty cash claim was made out for, say, £11.30 but mistakenly the amount given to the employee was £12.30.

♦ An employee borrowed £1 from the petty cash box for business expenses and this has not been recorded on a petty cash voucher.

♦ £1 has been stolen from the petty cash box.

Payroll procedures

1

	£
Gross pay	368.70
Less: PAYE	(46.45)
NIC	(23 96)
Net pay	298.29

2

Gross wages control account

	£		£
31 May Net pay – Bank	4,087	31 May Gross – wages expense	5,050
PAYE – Inland Revenue	635	31 May Emp'ers NIC – wages exp	425
Emp'ees NIC – Inland Rev	328		
Empl'ers NIC – Inland Rev	425		
	5,475		5,475

Wages expense account

	£		£
30 Apr Balance b/d	23,446		
31 May Gross – wages control	5,050		
Emp'ers NIC – control	425	31 May Balance c/d	28,921
	28,921		28,921
31 May Balance b/d	28,921		

Inland Revenue account

	£		£
19 May CPB	760	30 Apr Balance b/d	760
		31 May PAYE – wages control	635
		Emp'ees NIC – control	328
31 May Balance c/d	1,388	Emp'ers NIC – control	425
	2,148		2,148
		31 May Balance b/d	1,388

PRACTICE DEVOLVED ASSESSMENT 2
NATURAL PRODUCTS LTD

TASK 1

PURCHASE DAY BOOK

30/1/X1

Code	Supplier	Invoice no	Total		151		152		153		154		VAT	
B103	Bruning & Soler	111333	659	82			561	55					98	27
D101	Dehlavi Kosmetatos	111334	471	28					402	29			68	99
E103	James Ellington	111335	115	26							98	10	17	16
		111336	811	57			499	10			191	60	120	87
G103	Greig Handling	111337	308	11	262	22							45	89
H102	Hartley Chemicals	111338	563	30	479	41							83	89
		111339	87	90	74	81							13	09
M102	Mortimer, Hassell	111340	211	80			180	26					31	54
		111341	938	90	799	07							139	83
N101	Natural Ingredients	111342	1,381	33	1,175	60							205	73
	Totals		5,549	27	2,791	11	1,240	91	402	29	289	70	825	26

TASK 2

PURCHASE RETURNS DAY BOOK

30/1/X1

Code	Supplier	Credit note no	Total		161		162		163		164		VAT	
G103	Greig Handling	6273	35	19	29	95							5	24
M102	Mortimer, Hassell	6274	80	72			68	70					12	02
	Totals		115	91	29	95	68	70	-	-	-	-	17	26

TASK 3

SUBSIDIARY (PURCHASES) LEDGER ACCOUNTS

Supplier	Bruning & Soler Ltd				Account number		B103	
Address								
Telephone								
Date	**Transaction**	**£**		**Date**	**Transaction**	**£**		
8/1/X1	Cash	329	50	1/1/X1	b/f	329	50	
				30/1/X1	Inv 111333	659	82	

Supplier	Dehlavi Kosmetatos				Account number		D101	
Address								
Telephone								
Date	**Transaction**	**£**		**Date**	**Transaction**	**£**		
3/1/X1	Cash	645	10	1/1/X1	b/f	656	30	
	Discount	11	20	30/1/X1	Inv 111334	471	28	
30/1/X1	Cash	463	24					
	Discount	8	04					

SUBSIDIARY (PURCHASES) LEDGER ACCOUNTS

Supplier	Greig Handling (Import) Ltd			Account number	G103		
Address							
Telephone							
Date	**Transaction**	**£**		**Date**	**Transaction**	**£**	
8/1/X1	Cash	25	68	1/1/X1	b/f	25	68
30/1/X1	Cr note 6273	35	19	8/1/X1	Inv 110990	119	50
				30/1/X1	Inv 111337	308	11

Supplier	Hartley Chemicals Ltd			Account number	H102		
Address							
Telephone							
Date	**Transaction**	**£**		**Date**	**Transaction**	**£**	
1/1/X1	b/f	55	60	30/1/X1	Inv 111338	563	30
					Inv 111339	87	90

SUBSIDIARY (PURCHASES) LEDGER ACCOUNTS

Supplier	Mortimer, Hassell & Co				Account number	M102	

Address

Telephone

Date	Transaction	£		Date	Transaction	£	
30/1/X1	Cr note 6274	80	72	8/1/X1	Inv 110989	811	30
				30/1/X1	Inv 111340	211	80
				30/1/X1	Inv 111341	938	90

Supplier	Natural Ingredients Ltd				Account number	N101	

Address

Telephone

Date	Transaction	£		Date	Transaction	£	
30/1/X1	Cash	134	13	15/1/X1	Inv 110999	135	87
	Discount	1	74	30/1/X1	Inv 111342	1,381	33

SUBSIDIARY (PURCHASES) LEDGER ACCOUNTS

Supplier	Rendell & Sayers			Account number		R102	
Address							
Telephone							
Date	**Transaction**	**£**		**Date**	**Transaction**	**£**	
8/1/X1	Cash	246	26	1/1/X1	b/f	248	41
	Discount	2	12				

Supplier	James Ellington			Account number		E103	
Address							
Telephone							
Date	**Transaction**	**£**		**Date**	**Transaction**	**£**	
				30/1/X1	Inv 111335	115	26
					Inv 111336	811	57

TASK 4

		Journal no	1313		
		Date	5/2/X1		
		Prepared by	A N Other		

Code	Account	Debit		Credit	
151	Oils & Waxes	2,791	11		
152	Essential Oils	1,240	91		
153	Emulsifiers & Pres	402	29		
154	Colours	289	70		
022	VAT Control	825	26		
020	Trade Creditors			5,549	27
TOTALS		5,549	27	5,549	27

Narrative
To post totals from purchase day book (week ending 30 January 20X1).

TASK 5

268

Code	Account	Debit		Credit	
				Journal no	1314
				Date	5/2/X1
				Prepared by	A N Other
020	Trade Creditors	115	91		
161	Oils and Waxes			29	95
162	Essential Oils			68	70
022	VAT Control			17	26
TOTALS		115	91	115	91

Narrative
To post totals from purchase returns day book (week ending 30 January 20X1).

MAIN LEDGER

Account name	Oils & Waxes		Account no	151	
Narrative	£		Narrative	£	
23/1/X1 b/f	202,511	60			
30/1/X1 PDB 1313	2,791	11			

Account name	Essential Oils			Account no 152		
Narrative	£		Narrative	£		
23/1/X1 b/f	112,388	71				
30/1/X1 PDB 1313	1,240	91				

Account name	Emulsifiers & Preservatives			Account no 153		
Narrative	£		Narrative	£		
23/1/X1 b/f	50,115	90				
30/1/X1 PDB 1313	402	29				

Account name	Colours			Account no 154		
Narrative	£		Narrative	£		
23/1/X1 b/f	23,905	20				
30/1/X1 PDB 1313	289	70				

Account name	Trade creditors				Account no	020	
Narrative		£		Narrative		£	
3/1/X1	Cash 1-2	14,204	17	1/1/X1	b/f	28,958	33
	Discount 1-2	217	27				
8/1/X1	Cash 1-3	12,857	77	8/1/X1	Invoices 1-4	7,335	56
	Discount 1-3	80	53				
15/1/X1	Credit notes 1-7	203	60	15/1/X1	Invoices 1-6	6,201	38
30/1/X1	Cash 1-12	14,995	60	23/1/X1	Adjustment 1-8	711	60
	Discount 1-12	113	80	30/1/X1	Invoices 1313	5,549	27
	Credit notes 1314	115	91				

Account name	VAT Control Account				Account no	022	
Narrative		£		Narrative		£	
30/1/X1	PDB 1313	825	26	23/1/X1	b/f	5,311	90
				30/1/X1	PRDB 1314	17	26

Account name	Purchase Returns – Oils & Waxes		Account no	161	
Narrative	£		Narrative	£	
			23/1/X1 b/f	6,395	48
			30/1/X1 PRDB 1314	29	95

Account name	Purchases Returns – Essential Oils		Account no	162	
Narrative	£		Narrative	£	
			23/1/X1 b/f	3,125	24
			30/1/X1 PRDB 1314	68	70

Account name	Purchases Returns – Emulsifiers and Preservatives		Account no	163	
Narrative	£		Narrative	£	
			23/1/X1 b/f	1,486	07

Account name	Purchases Returns – Colours		Account no	164	
Narrative	£		Narrative	£	
			23/1/X1 b/f	1,375	33

TASK 6

DEHLAVI KOSMETATOS

388 Commercial Road Bristol BS1 3UH
Tel: 01272 755644

STATEMENT OF ACCOUNT

Customer name	Natural Products Ltd	Customer account no 090

Customer address 151 Green Lane
Taunton
TA20 6GH

Statement date 31 January 20X1		DR		CR		Balance	
Date	**Transaction**	**£**	**p**	**£**	**p**	**£**	**p**
1/1/X1	Balance brought forward	656	30			656	30
4/1/X1	Payment - thank you			645	10	11	20
24/1/X1	Invoice 2356	471	28			482	48
30/1/X1	Invoice 2389	399	40			881	88
Balance						**881**	**88**

	£
Balance per statement	881.88
Less: Goods in transit	(399.40)
Cash in transit	(463.24)
Discount on cash in transit	(8.04)
Discount not recorded on statement	(11.20)
Balance per creditors' ledger	Nil

Practice devolved assessment 4 - answers*

PRACTICE DEVOLVED ASSESSMENT 4

JP HARTNELL LTD (2)

TASK 1

Invoices received

Brown and Hargraves Ltd

English Gas plc

English Telecomm plc

H Freeman Timber Suppliers   unauthorised

Hardy Supplies Ltd   calculation error (invoice 12701)

Newman and Royston Ltd

Original Brass Fitting Company Ltd   calculation error (invoice 74378) - VAT

Parker and Fellows Supplies

TASK 2

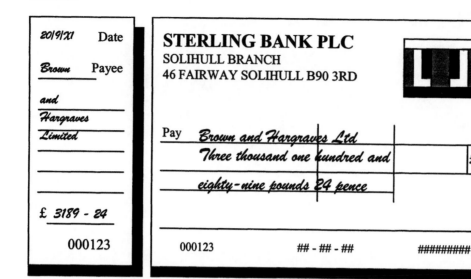

20/9/X1	Date
Brown	Payee
and	
Hargraves	
Limited	
£ 3189 - 24	
000123	

STERLING BANK PLC
SOLIHULL BRANCH
46 FAIRWAY SOLIHULL B90 3RD

- ## -
20/9/20X1

Pay   *Brown and Hargraves Ltd*   or order
         Three thousand one hundred and   £ 3189 - 24
         eighty-nine pounds 24 pence
                                                 J P HARTNELL LTD

000123   ## - ## - ##   #########

20/9/X1	Date
	Payee
English	
Gas	
plc	
£ 116 - 57	
000124	

STERLING BANK PLC
SOLIHULL BRANCH
46 FAIRWAY SOLIHULL B90 3RD

- ## -
20/9/20X1

Pay   *English Gas plc*   or order
         One hundred and sixteen pounds   £ 116 - 57
         57 pence only
                                                 J P HARTNELL LTD

000124   ## - ## - #   #########

20/9/X1	Date
	Payee
English	
Telecomm	
plc	
£ 138 - 22	
000125	

STERLING BANK PLC
SOLIHULL BRANCH
46 FAIRWAY SOLIHULL B90 3RD

- ## -
20/9/20X1

Pay   *English Telecomm plc*   or order
         One hundred and thirty-eight pounds   £ 138 - 22
         22 pence only
                                                 J P HARTNELL LTD

000125   ## - ## - ##   #########

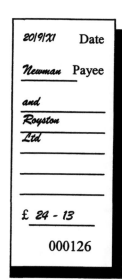
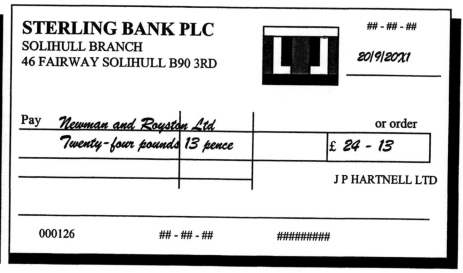

20/9/X1 Date	
Newman Payee	
and	
Royston	
Ltd	
£ *24 - 13*	
000126	

STERLING BANK PLC
SOLIHULL BRANCH
46 FAIRWAY SOLIHULL B90 3RD

- ## -
20/9/20X1

Pay   *Newman and Royston Ltd*   or order
      Twenty-four pounds 13 pence   £ *24 - 13*

J P HARTNELL LTD

000126   ## - ## - ##   #########

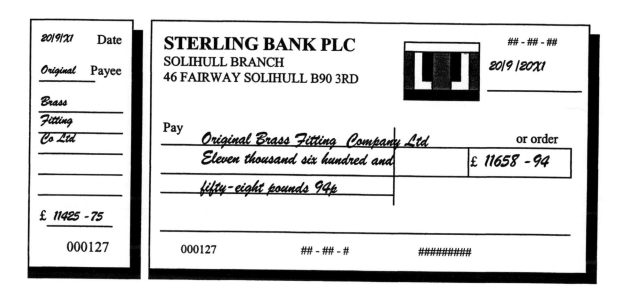

20/9/X1 Date	
Original Payee	
Brass	
Fitting	
Co Ltd	
£ *11425 -75*	
000127	

STERLING BANK PLC
SOLIHULL BRANCH
46 FAIRWAY SOLIHULL B90 3RD

- ## -
20/9 /20X1

Pay   *Original Brass Fitting Company Ltd*   or order
      Eleven thousand six hundred and   £ *11658 - 94*
      fifty-eight pounds 94p

000127   ## - ## - #   #########

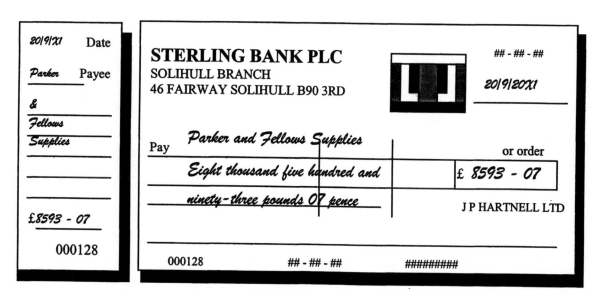

20/9/X1 Date	
Parker Payee	
&	
Fellows	
Supplies	
£*8593 - 07*	
000128	

STERLING BANK PLC
SOLIHULL BRANCH
46 FAIRWAY SOLIHULL B90 3RD

- ## -
20/9/20X1

Pay   *Parker and Fellows Supplies*   or order
      Eight thousand five hundred and   £ *8593 - 07*
      ninety-three pounds 07 pence

J P HARTNELL LTD

000128   ## - ## - ##   #########

TASK 3

Date	20/9/X1	Cheques Paid Listing		Site		Solihull	
Number	95			Prepared by		AN Other	

Supplier	Invoice No	Cheque No	Amount £		Discount taken £	
Brown and Hargraves Ltd	114598	123	3189	24		
English Gas plc	29/8/X1	124	116	57		
English Telecomm plc	6/9/X1	125	138	22		
Newman and Royston Ltd	457	126	24	13	0	37
Original Brass Fitting Company Ltd	74184, 74183	127	11658	94	202	50
Parker and Fellows Supplies	6679	128	8593	07	149	25
		Total	23720	17	352	12

TASK 4

REMITTANCE ADVICE

From: **JP Hartnell Ltd**
   Thelwell Works
   Thelwell Road
   Solihull B90 0AY **Tel: 0121 667 3993**

To: *Brown & Hargraves Ltd*

Date: *20/9/X1*

Details of invoices, etc	Amount	
Invoice N4598	3,189	24
Cheque no *123* enclosed	3,189	24

REMITTANCE ADVICE

From: **JP Hartnell Ltd**
   Thelwell Works
   Thelwell Road
   Solihull B90 0AY **Tel: 0121 667 3993**

To: *Newman & Royston Ltd*

Date: *20/9/X1*

Details of invoices, etc	Amount	
Invoice 457	24	50
Discount	(0	37)
Cheque no *126* enclosed	24	13

REMITTANCE ADVICE

From: **JP Hartnell Ltd**
   Thelwell Works
   Thelwell Road
   Solihull B90 0AY **Tel: 0121 667 3993**

To: *Original Brass Fitting Company Ltd*

Date: *20/9/X1*

Details of invoices, etc	Amount	
Invoice 74184	4,744	58
Discount	(81	00)
Invoice 74183	7,116	86
Discount	(121	50)
Cheque no *127* enclosed	11,658	94

REMITTANCE ADVICE		
From: **JP Hartnell Ltd** **Thelwell Works** **Thelwell Road** **Solihull B90 0AY** **Tel: 0121 667 3993** To: *Parker & Fellows Supplies* Date: *20/9/X1*		
Details of invoices, etc	Amount	
Invoice 6679	8,742	32
Discount	(149	25)
Cheque no *128* enclosed	8,593	07

TASK 5

What should happen to invoices which are

(a)   not authorised?

The numbers should be noted and the invoices returned to Paul Snow.

(b)   not coded?

Again the numbers should be noted and the invoices returned to Paul Snow.

(c)   inaccurate?

They should be kept in a discrepancies file. The supplier should be contacted to settle the matter and to arrange for a credit note.

TASK 6

You have drawn up a batch of cheques ready for signature, but one of the directors is on holiday. Suggest an alternative procedure for cheque signing in such circumstances.

Another person could be authorised to sign cheques for a limited period only.

TASK 7

Cheques prepared are sent with the **cheques paid listing** for signature. Why is the list sent as well?

So that the cheque signatory can check the recording of the cheque payments and the sequence of the cheques.

Suggest one way in which Paul Snow could check that all the cheques written are recorded on the listing.

He could total the amounts on the cheques and compare this to the total on the listing.

(This is a check which you should have performed after completing the listing.)

TASK 8

In writing out one of the cheques you have made an error. How must you deal with the cheque?

The cheque must be cancelled across its face, stored in a safe and marked as cancelled on the cheques paid listing.

TASK 9

Hardy Supplies Ltd
228 Thornton Lane
London
W12 9ER

J P Hartnell Ltd
Thelwell Works
       Thelwell Road
Solihull   B90 0AY

20 September 20X1

Dear Sir

Re: Invoice no 12701

I would like to draw your attention to the calculations on this invoice. The goods total should be £3,350 not £3,650 although the VAT is correct. Please send a credit note for the difference, £300.

Yours faithfully

Paul Snow
Finance Manager

Original Brass Fitting Co Ltd
63 Hollowtree Road
Wallsend
Newcastle   NE23 6TY

J P Hartnell Ltd
Thelwell Works
Thelwell Road
Solihull   B90 0AY

20 September 20X1

Dear Sir

Re: Invoice no 74378

I would like to draw your attention to the incorrect calculation of the VAT on this invoice. The correct amount of VAT should be £347.28. Please send us an amended invoice.

Yours faithfully

Paul Snow
Finance Manager

PRACTICE DEVOLVED ASSESSMENT 6
NATURAL PRODUCTS LIMITED (2)

TASK 1

CHEQUE REQUISITION			
Date:	29/6/X1	Voucher No:	340
Amount:	£235.55	Discount:	
Payee:	Arthur Chong Limited		
For trade creditors, account no: C102			
Purpose:	TC		
Signed:	Trudi Roberts	Authorised:	SAR
Payment date:	30/6/X1	Cheque No:	401

CHEQUE REQUISITION			
Date:	29/6/X1	Voucher No:	341
Amount:	£469.55	Discount:	£23.48
Payee:	Dwyer & Company (Import) Limited		
For trade creditors, account no: D102			
Purpose:	TC		
Signed:	Trudi Roberts	Authorised:	SAR
Payment date:	30/6/X1	Cheque No:	402

CHEQUE REQUISITION			
Date:	29/6/X1	Voucher No:	342
Amount:	£449.28	Discount:	£4.49
Payee:	Eastworld Ltd		
For trade creditors, account no: E101			
Purpose:	TC		
Signed:	Trudi Roberts	Authorised:	SAR
Payment date:	30/6/X1	Cheque No:	403

SOUTHERN BANK PLC
755 HIGH STREET TAUNTON TA1 4JL

22 - 56 - 01

_30|6_   **20X1**

Pay   *Arthur Chong Ltd*   or order

Two hundred and thirty five pounds | £235.55 |

and 55 pence only

FOR AND ON BEHALF OF
NATURAL PRODUCTS LTD

000401   22- 56 - 01   00010990

SOUTHERN BANK PLC
755 HIGH STREET TAUNTON TA1 4JL

22 - 56 - 01

_30|6_   **20X1**

Pay   *Dwyer & Company (Import) Limited*   or order

Four hundred and sixty nine pounds | £469.55 |

and 55 pence only

FOR AND ON BEHALF OF
NATURAL PRODUCTS LTD

000402   22- 56 - 01   00010990

SOUTHERN BANK PLC
755 HIGH STREET TAUNTON TA1 4JL

22 - 56 - 01

_30|6_   **20X1**

Pay   *Eastworld Limited*   or order

Four hundred and forty nine pounds | £449.28 |

and 28 pence only

FOR AND ON BEHALF OF
NATURAL PRODUCTS LTD

000403   22- 56 - 01   00010990

TASK 2

Cash Book Payments

Date	Narrative	Cheque no	Total £	Creditors £	Salaries £	Other £	VAT control £	Discount received £
26/6	Blackwood Foodstuffs	389	325.99	325.99				
	Bruning & Soler	390	683.85	683.85				
	Dehlavi Kosmetatos	391	2,112.16	2,112.16				
	Environmentally Friendly	392	705.77	705.77				
	Greig Handling (Import) Ltd	393	1,253.98	1,253.98				
	Halpern Freedman	394	338.11	338.11				
	Kobo Design Studio	395	500.00	500.00				
	Rayner Food Co	396	375.22	375.22				
	Year 2000 Produce Co	397	1,100.68	1,100.68				
27/6	HM Customs & Excise	398	23,599.28				23,599.28	
26/6	Petty Cash	399	175.10			175.10 (P cash)		
28/6	Salaries - Bank Giro	400	48,995.63		48,995.63			
30/6	Arthur Chong Ltd	401	235.55	235.55				
	Dwyer & Co (Import)Ltd	402	469.55	469.55				23.48
	Eastworld Ltd	403	449.28	449.28				4.49
	English Electricity	DD	159.78			135.98 (elec)	23.80	
	English Telecomm	DD	224.47			191.04 (Tele)	33.43	
	Totals		81,704.40	8,550.14	48,995.63	502.12	23,656.51	27.97

Note. As the amounts paid by direct debit are being recorded for the first time, the VAT must be analysed within the cash book. VAT is charged at standard rate on electricity and telephone charges and is therefore calculated as 17.5/117.5 of the amount paid.

TASK 3

All petty cash vouchers were correctly produced and will be paid. They will be numbered from 551 to 559.

TASK 4

Petty cash (payments)

Date	Voucher No	Total £	212 Bld Maint £	401 Staff welfare £	230 Motor expenses £	222 Travel & subs £	221 Stationery £	211 Repairs & renewals £	022 VAT £
30/6/X1	551	8.90	8.90						
	552	3.99		3.99					
	553	1.99			1.99				
	554	6.95				6.95			
	555	8.29		7.40					0.89
	556	12.98					12.98		
	557	5.99		5.49					0.50
	558	2.80				2.80			
	559	32.90						28.00	4.90
	Total	84.79	8.90	16.88	1.99	9.75	12.98	28.00	6.29

TASK 5

```
┌─────────────────────────────────────────────────────────────┐
│                PETTY CASH RECONCILIATION                      │
│                                                               │
│  Date:  6/7/X1              Prepared by:      AN Other         │
│                                                               │
│                             Authorised by:                    │
│                                                      £        │
│  Cash per petty cash book                                     │
│        Balance brought forward 23/6                 24.90     │
│        Receipts                                    175.10     │
│        Payments                                    (84.79)    │
│                                                  ─────────    │
│        Balance carried forward 30/6                115.21     │
│                                                  ─────────    │
│  Cash in hand                                      115.21     │
│                                                  ─────────    │
│  Difference                                          —        │
│                                                  ─────────    │
└─────────────────────────────────────────────────────────────┘
```

The imprest level is given as £200. Therefore, the balance brought forward is £200 - £175.10 (the petty cash cheque made out on 26/6).

TASK 6

```
┌─────────────────────────────────────────────────────────────┐
│                   CHEQUE REQUISITION                          │
│                                                               │
│  Date:        6/7/X1                  Voucher No:             │
│  Amount:      £84.79                  Discount:               │
│  Payee:       Petty cash                                      │
│  For trade creditors, account no:                             │
│  Purpose:     Imprest                                         │
│                                                               │
│                                                               │
│  Signed:      AN Other                Authorised:            │
│  Payment date:                        Cheque No:             │
└─────────────────────────────────────────────────────────────┘
```

TASK 7

		Journal no	6111		
		Date	30/6/X1		
		Prepared by	A N Other		

Code	Account	Debit		Credit	
020	Trade creditors	8,550	14		
201	Wages and salaries	48,995	63		
014	Cash in hand	175	10		
208	Heat and light	135	98		
209	Telephones	191	04		
022	VAT control	23,656	51		
012	Cash at bank (Current)			81,704	40
020	Trade creditors	27	97		
144	Discounts received			27	97
Total		81,732	37	81,732	37

Narrative

To record cash payments (totals)

TASK 8

		Journal no	6112
		Date	30/6/X1
		Prepared by	A N Other

Code	Account	Debit		Credit	
022	VAT control	6	29		
212	Building maintenance	8	90		
401	Staff welfare	16	88		
230	Motor expenses	1	99		
222	Travel & subsistence	9	75		
221	Stationery	12	98		
211	Repairs and renewals	28	00		
014	Cash in hand			84	79
Total		84	79	84	79

Narrative

To record petty cash payments

TASK 9

MAIN LEDGER

Account Name: *Discounts received*		Account No: 144	
Narrative	£	*Narrative*	£
		23/6/X1 b/f 30/6/X1 6111	25,651.48 27.97

Account Name: *Wages and salaries*		Account No: 201	
Narrative	£	*Narrative*	£
31/5/X1 b/f 30/6/X1 6111	325,119.90 48,995.63		

Account Name: *Heat and Light*		Account No: 208	
Narrative	£	*Narrative*	£
23/6/X1 b/f 30/6/X1 6111	12,995.65 135.98		

Account Name: *Telephones*		Account No: 209	
Narrative	£	*Narrative*	£
23/6/X1 b/f 30/6/X1 6111	3,225.91 191.04		

Account Name: *Repairs and renewals*		Account No: 211	
Narrative	£	Narrative	£
31/5/X1 b/f 30/6/X1 6112	2,001.68 28.00		

Account Name: *Building maintenance*		Account No: 212	
Narrative	£	Narrative	£
28/2/X1 b/f 30/6/X1 6112	1,500.74 8.90		

Account Name: *Stationery*		Account No: 221	
Narrative	£	Narrative	£
23/6/X1 b/f 30/6/X1 6112	8,020.97 12.98		

Account Name: *Travel and subsistence*		Account No: 222	
Narrative	£	Narrative	£
23/6/X1 b/f 30/6/X1 6112	10,255.65 9.75		

Account Name: *Motor expenses*		Account No: 230	
Narrative	£	*Narrative*	£
16/6/X1 b/f	*5,885.94*		
30/6/X1 6112	*1.99*		

Account Name: *Staff welfare*		Account No: 401	
Narrative	£	*Narrative*	£
23/6/X1 b/f	*4,110.28*		
30/6/X1 6112	*16.88*		

Account Name: *Cash at bank (current)*		Account No: 012	
Narrative	£	*Narrative*	£
23/6/X1 b/f	*84,579.77*	*30/6/X1*	*81,704.40*

Account Name: *Cash in hand*		Account No: 014	
Narrative	£	*Narrative*	£
23/6/X1 b/f	*24.90*	*30/6/X1 6112*	*84.79*
30/6/X1 6111	*175.10*		

Account Name: *Trade creditors*		Account No: 020	
Narrative	£	*Narrative*	£
30/6/X1 6111	*8,550.14*	*23/6/X1 b/f*	*367,251.44*
30/6/X1 6111	*27.97*		

Account Name: *VAT control account*		Account No: 022	
Narrative	£	*Narrative*	£
30/6/X1 6111	*23,656.51*	*23/6/X1 b/f*	*22,987.38*
30/6/X1 6112	*6.29*		

AAT UNIT 2

MOCK DEVOLVED ASSESSMENT 2

SEAMER RETAIL LTD

ANSWERS

ANSWERS - PART ONE, TASK 1

Petty Cash Voucher	Folio _____ Date _____

For what required	AMOUNT	
	£	p
Stationery	11	10
	11	10

Signature	Adam Haynes
Passed by	

Petty Cash Voucher	Folio ____175____ Date ____7/11/X1

For what required	AMOUNT	
	£	p
Stationery	6	95
	6	95

Signature	Adam Haynes
Passed by	A Student

Petty Cash Voucher	Folio _____ Date _____

For what required	AMOUNT	
	£	p
Stationery	4	94
	4	94

Signature	Adam Haynes
Passed by	

Petty Cash Voucher	Folio ____176_____ Date ____7/11/X1

For what required	AMOUNT	
	£	p
Stationery	7	33
	7	33

Signature	Adam Haynes
Passed by	A Student

Petty Cash Voucher	Folio _____ Date _____

For what required	AMOUNT	
	£	p
Stationery	15	35
	15	35

Signature	Adam Haynes
Passed by	

Petty Cash Voucher	Folio _____ Date _____

For what required	AMOUNT	
	£	p
Stamps	12	35
	12	35

Signature	Jane Hawkins
Passed by	

ANSWERS - PART ONE, TASK 1 (CONTINUED)

Petty Cash Voucher	Folio	177
	Date	7/11/X1

For what required	AMOUNT £	p
Stamps	5	25
	5	25

Signature	*Jane Hawkins*
Passed by	A Student

Petty Cash Voucher	Folio	178
	Date	7/11/X1

For what required	AMOUNT £	p
Stamps	3	94
	3	94

Signature	*Jane Hawkins*
Passed by	A Student

Petty Cash Voucher	Folio	179
	Date	7/11/X1

For what required	AMOUNT £	p
Stamps	0	76
	0	76

Signature	*Jane Hawkins*
Passed by	A Student

Petty Cash Voucher	Folio	180
	Date	7/11/X1

For what required	AMOUNT £	p
Taxi fare (meeting with auditors)	5	20
	5	20

Signature	*Gillian Russell*
Passed by	A Student

Petty Cash Voucher	Folio	181
	Date	7/11/X1

For what required	AMOUNT £	p
Taxi fare (meeting with supplier)	6	10
	6	10

Signature	*Ben Thornley*
Passed by	A Student

ANSWERS - PART ONE, TASK 1, CONTINUED

MEMORANDUM OF DISCREPANCIES
FOR LETTER TO GILLIAN RUSSELL

Details of claim	Action
Stationery Supplies Receipt *3 Nov X1 Adam Haynes* *Total £15.35*	*Above my limit for authorisation.* *G Russell to authorise.*
Petty Cash Voucher *From Adam Haynes for stationery* *£4.94*	*No corresponding receipt to process.* *Wait for relevant receipt*
Stamps from Jane Hawkins *£12.35*	*Above my limit for authorisation.* *G Russell to authorise.*
Stationery from Adam Haynes *£11.10*	*Above my limit for authorisation.* *G Russell to authorise.*

ANSWERS – PART ONE, TASK 2

PETTY CASH BOOK

Receipts	Date	Details	Voucher	Total	VAT	Travel	Stationery	PCB22 Postage
£	20X1			£	£	£	£	£
100.00	31-Oct	Balance b/d						
	7 11 X1	Stationery Supp.	175	6 95	1.03		5 92	
	7.11 X1	Stationery Supp.	176	7 33	1 09		6 24	
	7.11.X1	Stamps	177	5.25				5.25
	7.11.X1	Stamps	178	3.94				3.94
	7.11.X1	Stamps	179	0.76				0.76
	7.11.X1	Taxi	180	5.20	0.77	4.43		
	7.11.X1	Taxi	181	6.10	0.91	5.19		
				35.53	3.80	9.62	12.16	9.95
35.53	7.11.X1	Cash to restore						
	7.11.X1	Bal c/f		100.00				

ANSWERS - PART ONE, TASK 3

PETTY CASH BOX

			£
£10	× 4	=	40.00
£5	× 3	=	15.00
£1	× 6	=	6.00
50p	× 3	=	1.50
20p	× 4	=	.80
10p	× 9	=	.90
2p	× 8	=	.16
1p	× 11	=	.11
Total			£64.47

RECONCILIATION OF PETTY CASH

Petty Cash Book

	£
Opening balance of imprest	100.00
Payments	(35.53)
Closing balance	64.47
Cash counted	64.46

ANSWERS - PART TWO, TASK 4

REMITTANCE ADVICE

From: **Seamer Retail Limited**
37 Cain Road
Scarborough
YO12 4HF

To: *Baxley Limited*
Station Road
Horsford
TV12 3EW

Date: *7 Nov X1*

Details	Amount £	p
Invoice No 4132 dated 26/10/X1		
Goods	1,788	56
VAT	309	86
Cheque no 305082 enclosed	2,098	42

In case of query, please contact *A Student / G Russell*

7/11/X1 Date
Baxley Payee
Limited

£2098.42

305082

Wadsworth Bank Plc
Chambers Street, Scarborough YO12 3NZ

25-46-70

7 Nov 20X1

Pay Baxley Limited only

Two thousand and ninety-eight pounds and 42p

£2098.42

For Seamer Retail Ltd

305082 25-46-70 21758391

ANSWERS - PART TWO, TASK 4, CONTINUED

REMITTANCE ADVICE

From: **Seamer Retail Limited**
            37 Cain Road
            Scarborough
            YO12 4HF

To: *Harborne Limited*
            12 Barton Street
            Apton AN3 4RT

Date: 7 Nov X1

Details		Amount	
		£	p
Invoice No 2541 dated 7/10/X1			
	Goods	2,076	22
	VAT	363	33
Cheque no 305083 enclosed		2,439	55

In case of query, please contact   *A Student / G Russell*

7/11/X1   Date
_____ Payee
Harborne
Limited
_____
_____
_____
£2439.55
305083

Wadsworth Bank Plc   25-46-70
Chambers Street, Scarborough YO12 3NZ

                                              7 Nov   20X1

Pay   Harborne Limited   only

          Two thousand four hundred and   £2439.55

          thirty-nine pounds and 55p

                                              For Seamer Retail Ltd

305083   25-46-70   21758391

ANSWERS - PART TWO, TASK 4, CONTINUED

REMITTANCE ADVICE

From: **Seamer Retail Limited**
   37 Cain Road
   Scarborough
   YO12 4HF

To: *Hurley Limited*
   241 Steels Avenue
   Picton SR5 9TY

Date: 7 Nov X1

Details		Amount £	p
Invoice No 1008 dated 1/10/X1			
	Goods	300	17
	VAT	52	52
Cheque no 305084 enclosed		352	69

In case of query, please contact   *A Student / G Russell*

7/11/X1 Date

Hurley Payee
Limited

£352.69

305084

Wadsworth Bank Plc
Chambers Street, Scarborough YO12 3NZ

25-46-70

7 Nov   20X1

Pay   Hurley Limited   only

Three hundred and fifty-two pounds

and 69p

£352.69

For Seamer Retail Ltd

305084   25-46-70   21758391

ANSWERS - PART TWO, TASK 4, CONTINUED

REMITTANCE ADVICE

From: **Seamer Retail Limited**
           37 Cain Road
           Scarborough
           YO12 4HF

To: *Allen and Banks*
           49 Exley Road
           Traxham TM5 1UJ

Date: **7 Nov X1**

Details		Amount £	p
Invoice No 1673 dated 27/10/X1			
	Goods	654	08
	Discount	(9	81)
	VAT	112	74
Cheque no 305085 enclosed		757	01

In case of query, please contact   *A Student / G Russell*

<u>7/11/X1</u>   Date
 	
Allen   Payee
and Banks
―――――――
Discount taken
£9.81
―――――――
―――――――
<u>£757.01</u>
 	
305085
	Wadsworth Bank Plc 25-46-70
	Chambers Street, Scarborough YO12 3NZ
	
	                  <u>7 Nov</u> <u>20X1</u>
	
	Pay Allen and Banks only
	
	   <u>Seven hundred and fifty</u> £757.01
	   <u>seven pounds and 01p</u>
	                         For Seamer Retail Ltd
	
	   305085 25-46-70 21758391

ANSWERS - PART TWO, TASK 4, CONTINUED

REMITTANCE ADVICE

From: **Seamer Retail Limited**
        37 Cain Road
        Scarborough
        YO12 4HF

To: *Wallace Limited*
        101-105 Knighton Road
        Brixley BY2 3FR

Date: 7 Nov X1

Details		Amount £	p
Invoice No 4321 dated 10/10/X1			
	Goods	102	66
	VAT	17	96
Cheque 305086 enclosed		120	62

In case of query, please contact   *A Student / G Russell*

7/11/X1 Date
Wallace   Payee
Limited
————
————
————
————
£120.62
305086

Wadsworth Bank Plc   25-46-70
Chambers Street, Scarborough YO12 3NZ

                                7 Nov   20X1

Pay   Wallace Limited   only

    One hundred and twenty pounds   £120.62

    and 62p   For Seamer Retail Ltd

305086   25-46-70   21758391

ANSWERS - PART TWO, TASK 5

CASH BOOK PAYMENTS

							CPB 53
Date	Payee/details	Cheque no	Total	VAT	Creditors	Discount Received	Sundry
20X1			£	£	£	£	£
7 Nov	Petty Cash	305081	35.53				35.53
7 Nov	Baxley Ltd Inv 4132	305082	2,098.42		2,098.42		
7 Nov	Harborne Ltd Inv 2541	305083	2,439.55		2,439.55		
7 Nov	Hurley Ltd Inv 1008	305084	352.69		352.69		
7 Nov	Allen & Banks Inv 1673	305085	757.01		757.01	9.81	
7 Nov	Wallace Ltd Inv 4321	305086	120.62		120.62		
			5,803.82		5,768.29	9.81	35.53

ANSWERS - PART THREE, TASK 6

MAIN LEDGER

Account *Postage*

Date 20X1	Details	Amount £	Date 20X1	Details	Amount £
31-Oct	Bal b/f	213.76			
7 Nov	Petty Cash Book	9.95			

Debit — Credit

Account **Stationery** Debit				Credit	
Date 20X1	Details	Amount £	Date 20X1	Details	Amount £
31-Oct 7 Nov	Bal b/f Petty Cash Book	543.09 12.16			

Account **Travel** Debit				Credit	
Date 20X1	Details	Amount £	Date 20X1	Details	Amount £
31-Oct 7 Nov	Bal b/f Petty Cash Book	513.88 9.62			

Account **Purchase ledger control** Debit				Credit	
Date 20X1	Details	Amount £	Date 20X1	Details	Amount £
7 Nov 7 Nov	Bank Discount received	5,768.29 9.81	31-Oct	Bal b/f	28,996.21

Account *VAT*

Date 20X1	Details	Amount £	Date 20X1	Details	Amount £
7 Nov	Petty Cash Book	3.80	31-Oct	Bal b/f	2,499.04

Debit / Credit

Account *Cash sales*

Date 20X1	Details	Amount £	Date 20X1	Details	Amount £
			31- Oct	Bal b/f	51,235.99

Debit / Credit

Account *Discount received*

Date 20X1	Details	Amount £	Date 20X1	Details	Amount £
			31-Oct	Bal b/f	147.39
			7- Nov	Purchase ledger control	9.81

Debit / Credit

ANSWERS - PART THREE, TASK 6, CONTINUED

SUBSIDIARY (PURCHASES) LEDGER

Account *Allen and Banks*
Debit / Credit

Date 20X1	Details	Amount £	Date 20X1	Details	Amount £
7 Nov	Bank	757.01	31-Oct	Bal b/f	1,152.90
7 Nov	Discount received	9.81			

Account *Baxley Limited*
Debit / Credit

Date 20X1	Details	Amount £	Date 20X1	Details	Amount £
7 Nov	Bank	2,098.42	31-Oct	Bal b/f	3,012.75

Account *Harborne Limited*
Debit / Credit

Date 20X1	Details	Amount £	Date 20X1	Details	Amount £
7 Nov	Bank	2,439.55	31-Oct	Bal b/f	3,225.67

ANSWERS - PART THREE, TASK 6, CONTINUED

SUBSIDIARY (PURCHASES) LEDGER

Account *Hurley Limited*

Debit			Credit		
Date 20X1	Details	Amount £	Date 20X1	Details	Amount £
7 Nov	Bank	352.69	31-Oct	Bal b/f	961.44

Account *Wallace Limited*

Debit			Credit		
Date 20X1	Details	Amount £	Date 20X1	Details	Amount £
7 Nov	Bank	120.62	31-Oct	Bal b/f	546.08

ANSWERS - PART THREE, TASK 7

MEMO

To: *Gillian Russell*

From: *A Student*

Subject: *Week ending 7 Nov X1   Discrepancies*

Date: *7 Nov X1*

The following discrepancies were found in the course of dealing with the Petty Cash:

Petty Cash claim from Adam Haynes for £4.94 for stationery was not processed as there was no corresponding receipt.

There were three vouchers/receipts which are awaiting your authorisation before processing.

A Student
